CATHY CODE

WHY NOT?

SURVIVE AND THRIVE

GREENLEAF
BOOK GROUP PRESS

This book is intended as a reference volume only. It is sold with the understanding that the publisher and author are not engaged in rendering any professional services. The information given here is designed to help you make informed decisions. If you suspect that you have a problem that might require professional treatment or advice, you should seek competent help.

Published by Greenleaf Book Group Press
Austin, Texas
www.gbgpress.com

Distributed by Greenleaf Book Group

For ordering information or special discounts for bulk purchases, please contact Greenleaf Book Group at PO Box 91869, Austin, TX 78709, 512.891.6100.

Design and composition by Greenleaf Book Group
Cover design by Greenleaf Book Group

Cataloging-in-Publication data is available.

ISBN: 978-1-62634-184-5
eBook ISBN: 978-1-62634-185-2

Part of the Tree Neutral® program, which offsets the number of trees consumed in the production and printing of this book by taking proactive steps, such as planting trees in direct proportion to the number of trees used: www.treeneutral.com

TreeNeutral

Printed in the United States of America on acid-free paper

15 16 17 18 19 20   10 9 8 7 6 5 4 3 2 1

First Edition

CONTENTS

CHAPTER 1

FROM THE ASHES, A BEGINNING

I was pushing a grocery cart through Costco when I got the call. My girls scrambled from the cart, where they liked to hang for the ride. They sensed something wasn't right. "Mom, what's wrong?" Carmen, who was ten and my oldest, quizzed.

"Oh, my God," I blurted out, unable to comprehend what I'd just been told. "It's our house. We've got to go now!" I grabbed the girls' hands and we ran to the parking lot, leaving a full shopping cart abandoned in the aisle.

My fingers tightened around the steering wheel when we turned onto Larch Street. I was afraid of what we might find. As I slowed, I was almost rear-ended by a noisy fire truck racing to join the other emergency vehicles stationed in the middle of the block.

It was true. The back of our house was on fire.

There were long, sputtering hoses, firemen running this way and that, groups of shocked neighbors gathering, and smoke. So much smoke.

Where were my dogs, Cody and Chloe? Where were my three cats? I wanted to run into the house, but the firemen forbade it. All I was allowed to do was watch helplessly.

Caitlin, my youngest daughter, who was only six, began to cry, until a kind fireman hoisted both of my girls up into the cab of a fire truck. There they sat safely, their faces pressed up against the window, Caitlin clutching a well-worn blankie—both witnessing all the commotion caused by our burning house.

Within one hour everything was gone. Every possession destroyed.

The good news was that my two dogs and three cats had been saved. Our black Labrador retrievers had made it out through the dog door and into the yard, and the fireman carried out the two tabbies and one black cat. They had been rescued, but nothing else had.

I held the smallest tabby in my arms as I tried to digest what had just happened. This had been our home for fifteen years, and now it was gutted and exposed to all. I'd had my babies in this house—now it was scorched and smoldering.

Only days before, workers had begun construction on a plan I'd put in place after many months of brainstorming: a bed-and-breakfast. My idea had been to start a business right there in my twenty-five-year-old house in Abbotsford, British Columbia.

The business was a bit of a risk. I did not own a charming Victorian home in the heart of some popular tourist village. My house was a modest split-level, and the town of Abbotsford, about an hour's drive east of Vancouver, was best known for its federal prison and international air show. There was nothing quaint about it. But this did not stop me. I was determined.

I decided to start by converting one room at the back of the house. Eventually, I hoped to convert the entire basement, garage, family room . . . and, who knew? If all went well, I'd add on more guest rooms.

To avoid any fuss, I told my husband, Larry, that I had the idea for tax purposes. We would be able to write off some of our home expenses. The truth was more than that.

I was becoming weary of Larry's ongoing education and years of night classes to earn his doctorate in education. And I was feeling beaten down by his reminders that I was "just a girl from the prairie." (I was born in rural Saskatchewan, in the heart of Canada's Prairie Provinces—a region of farmland, cattle ranches, windswept plains, and wheat fields.) "I'll agree to more schooling for you if I get to improve myself too," I told him.

Improving me meant finding a way to make money working from home. I'd taken a few college classes at night part-time, but it was a tough schedule. Larry was never home. He typed. He worked. He read. He did research at the library. I was expected to care for our daughters and help pay the bills, so I had to hire a babysitter if I was working or if I wanted to take a course. With two young girls, that was not so easy.

And that's how the bed-and-breakfast came to mind. It seemed like a brilliant solution at the time. I'd start a business in my home. I'd begin slowly, renovating one room at a time. I wouldn't have to pay a sitter.

So I got a bit of credit and set about making my bed-and-breakfast fantasy a reality. It wasn't a fancy dream, but it was huge for me. It was my security. And my exit strategy. If my marriage continued as it was, at least I would have a place where my daughters would be secure. I would have a way to make money.

That was my plan. But you know what they say about the best-laid plans. As it turned out, the workers who were hired to move the washer and dryer used a blowtorch on the plumbing. This caused the back wall to catch fire—a fire that ran up the walls into the utility room and on throughout the house. And with that, my future burst into flames.

I couldn't imagine that life could get worse.

But it did.

The fire restoration crew ripped everything out—carpets, blinds, everything—then they took every stick of furniture to a warehouse while they treated the home for smoke damage.

The renovation was to take two weeks. While our pets were allowed to stay in the backyard at the house if I brought them daily food, it was impossible for our family to remain inside. The insurance company provided us with a hotel.

And let me just say that this hotel was the type of place that was quite *active* at night.

The next thing you know, we discovered lice in Caitlin's long blonde hair. Carmen got an ear infection from the hotel pool. Then both girls came down with chicken pox. Both dogs got fleas because they were living in the backyard, going without regular baths. Larry was busy with his job and school and was gone from early morning until late at night.

One week went by. Two weeks. Three. We were in the hotel for three months. We were miserable.

The slow renovation stemmed from the fact that the insurance company would only repair what was damaged from the fire. They would not repair every wall, since we had been renovating for the bed-and-breakfast. *This* wall could be repaired. *That* wall could not. We had two sets of insurance companies, two sets of carpenters, and *nothing* was happening.

My belongings—everything from my underwear to my checkbook—had been carted off before I could see or sort through them. Lots of things went missing. And the insurance company didn't replace possessions at their original cost. For example, Ariel, Caitlin's favorite Disney bath toy, had retailed for $30. The insurance company's reimbursement was $1.99. And so began my first exposure to the complex world of insurance fraud.

I wondered how I could make it through another day. I was so discouraged that after Larry and the girls would leave for work and school in the morning, I would drive to the house to sit and cry. I felt vulnerable and alone, the dogs my only companions.

During those days, I had a lot of time to think about my life. It was then that I remembered another damaged home. I realized that my childhood home had been "on fire" too. In that house, there had been fiery arguments between my mom and dad, and smoldering resentments that both my younger sister and I felt toward our parents.

I was born in a very small town in Saskatchewan, Canada, a place called Birch Hills. During my first six years, Mom and Dad seemed happily married. I'm sure that others thought we had a charmed life. We lived in an upper-middle-class community and our neighborhood was nicknamed Snob Hill. Our 1960s house was spacious and had polished wooden floors, six bedrooms, and several bathrooms. But it was never a home. I didn't know anything different, but somehow—whether it was because of the tightness of Mom's mouth or the harsh tone in Dad's voice—things never felt quite right.

On the one hand, it seemed like Mom and Dad only wanted the best for us. My little sister, Brenda, and I loved the playroom, the ping-pong room, and my favorite place, the lounge. We pretended to be movie stars and dancers, strutting and swirling, with our mother as our audience. It seemed that we were destined for effortless greatness.

We had lots of things. My parents owned a two-seater airplane, nice cars, and a vacation cabin on the lake. But there was something missing among all the stuff—all the rooms, toys, and extravagances. Even as a young kid, my gut told me that something was terribly wrong.

My father and mother (then later, my uncle) ran the family bakery. My father's father, a German immigrant, had been a baker. The bakery stood on Main Street, which, in a town with a population of 125, consisted of a couple of stores and a school. The bakery was shaded by a large and graceful willow tree and occupied the bottom level of a two-story brick building. Before we moved thirty miles away to the bigger and fancier house, we lived on top of the bakery. My bedroom was in the back, right above the ovens. To this day, I can't stand the smell of freshly baked bread.

We made breads, hot cross buns, doughnuts. If it used flour, our family baked it. At 4:00 a.m., every day, the baking began. I was a happy helper and loved to assist my uncle in the early morning hours, rolling the dough and flipping the doughnuts. Even more, I loved to ride along with my uncle into the nearby town of Prince Albert, delivering the bread to grocery stores and restaurants.

My mother was a farm girl who married "the man from the city" with his own business. It was an opportunity for her to move away from home. I remember Mom as a beautiful lady, the perfect 1960s housewife, looking like a glamorous movie star. I can't imagine how many hours she spent molding her fiery red hair into a perfect French roll.

My father was ten years older than my mother; he was tall and lean. He sported the classic 1950s slicked-back dark hair. His dramatic eyebrows completed the look. He was handsome in his black suit, white shirt, and skinny black tie. His pearly smile caught lots of female attention.

I believed my Mom and Dad were made for each other. But like I said, there was a lot I didn't understand. Their marriage unraveled, and in the next three years, beginning when I was around six years old, our family life went from bad to worse. Dad had always been a conscientious worker, but he spent evenings sitting in his chair drinking cold beer. Or he didn't come home at all.

For nights on end, Brenda and I went to bed hearing muffled noises downstairs. At first we thought it was the television, but we eventually realized that our parents were fighting. Dad swore. Mom yelled. Doors slammed.

Sometime after my ninth birthday, Mom left. She did not explain much to me and Brenda. "I have to go," she told us. "But I promise I love you." We were numb and uncomprehending. Brenda and I stayed with Dad for six months.

Life became a living hell.

Dad threw chaotic drinking parties at our house. Middle-aged women walked in and out of bedrooms. Some I liked, some I didn't. One hung around more than the others. But to me, they were all strange women. I only wanted to know why *my mother* wasn't home. When was *she* coming back?

My sister and I tried our best to stay out of sight. And that wasn't too hard, since mostly, Dad was gone. When Dad was home, ear-pounding country music filled the house. Dad's guy friends whispered to each other. I watched him exchange handfuls of money for white powder. I knew this wasn't flour. I would stay home to take care of Brenda and household affairs. I didn't go to school for forty days.

Most nights I cried, wondering why my mother had left us, hoping she would come back to get us. "What kind of mother would leave her kids?" Dad said to us. "She's an evil woman."

The confidence and assurance I once had ebbed away every night. I lay awake wrestling with anxieties: Was I the problem? Had I done something wrong? Why didn't she love us anymore?

Dad was gone more and more, physically and emotionally. He wasn't capable of caring for his two daughters. My dad had become an alcoholic and a drug abuser. That meant that he cared about only one thing—himself. There was no food in the pantry. Brenda and I woke up hungry and went to bed with growling stomachs. I was a baker's daughter without a crumb to eat. Our clothes were tattered and worn, and they no longer fit. Winter arrived, and we didn't have good coats. The house was still big, though it was now in disarray and becoming shabby.

I knew that it had to be my job to take care of my younger sister. We had to fend for ourselves.

One day before Dad left for work, I saw him hiding money. I found his secret stash: a huge wad of cash in a brown lunch bag hidden under the mattress.

I took it. All of it.

Suddenly I had power, and I knew the money would help me change the way things were for me and Brenda. That's when it dawned on me that I could take control of my own life. I decided to change my circumstances. I was nine years old.

In a flash, Brenda and I jumped on a city bus, knowing that Dad wouldn't be home until late. We had a fantastic day. I bought a bag of groceries and a new thick winter coat for each of us. I purchased warm and fuzzy mittens, socks and shoes, the works. Now my sister and I had food, clothing, shoes that fit—nothing else seemed to matter.

I hadn't really thought through the inevitable consequences that I would face once my father returned home. He walked into the house and I tried to run, but he cornered me. I was a young thief and I was caught red-handed. Brenda and I were wearing the evidence, and seeing us in our new clothes made him furious. We had used every last penny for the return bus ride. The money was gone, money that he had planned to use to feed his raging addictions.

He took off his leather belt and the yelling began. My father's face was red-hot with rage. His wild, glassy eyes met mine and then he beat me with the belt. He had never done that before. As bad as things had been, he had seldom been angry with me. I felt the belt buckle break the skin. The shock and pain caused me to stiffen. The blows came quicker and harder, until suddenly, he stopped. "I hope you've learned your lesson," he said before storming off. I was too scared to answer or move. My backside was blistered, brutally bruised, and bloody. I will never forget lying on the floor, curled up and whimpering.

Though I didn't realize it then, my pain and fear were strengthening me like a blast furnace forging steel. I was an ordinary kid in an extraordinary circumstance; growing up fast, I had to figure out how to survive this nightmare, but there was more to it than that. My job was not just to survive. I wanted to be a kid again. I wanted to thrive.

The memories of that time, of that nine-year-old girl, were just that, memories. I wiped the sniffles and tears away with my crumpled tissue and looked around my now damaged home. In that moment, my attitude changed. It started with a small grin, which grew large and wide across my face. Before I knew it, I had begun to laugh: big, loud whoops of laughter. Yes, there had been a fire. But no one had been physically harmed. Everything could be replaced—eventually. Like that nine-year-old girl, I would need to take charge and change my current circumstances. It would require hard work, but hard work was something I could do.

I stood before my gutted house and pictured once more exactly how I wanted my bed-and-breakfast room to look. Modern and clean. It would be a home away from home for my many guests. This would be no impersonal, square box. I would make sure to include thoughtful touches and all the practical conveniences. There would be a small fridge and a microwave, and I would leave a basket filled with fruit, cereal, and hot cross buns.

When faced with a difficult choice in your life, will you let disappointment and thwarted plans stop you from creating the life you dream of? Can you reach back to your earliest memories, recalling who you are and where you come from? Can you draw on the unique inner strengths you possess, strengths that have the power to help you move forward and out of the rubble?

Disappointment and disheartenment can control you, or you can make the decision to use your energy to create something positive—to find one bit of hope to hold on to. Just one small action can change something that might feel insurmountable. You can begin to dismantle a mountainous obstacle by carrying away one small stone. That is a beginning.

EXERCISES

A. Clearly describe two significant circumstances in your life today that are difficult, unfair, or destructive.

1. _____

_____

_____

_____

2. _____

_____

_____

_____

B. Complete the sentence below using any number of simple and descriptive words like angry, frustrated, powerless, overwhelmed, tired, etc.

Today, because of my negative circumstance,

I feel _____ , _____ ,

_____ , and _____ .

Using two or three sentences for each of the feeling words you've mentioned above, describe WHY you feel this way today.

The reason I feel _____

is because _____ .

An example:

> "I felt completely discouraged and disheartened when my bed-and-breakfast burned to the ground. The reason I feel this way is because I've no idea how I'll make a living and provide a home for my children."

Taking only a moment to write down your circumstances and feelings (or talking about your circumstances and feelings) is the first step in making positive choices and helpful differences in your life. Baby steps!

CHAPTER 2

SURVIVAL INSTINCTS

It is a process to become our best self, to arrive at a point where we feel comfortable and secure with who we are. When we feel trapped in a dark place, we can become paralyzed, making it difficult to embrace change, making it overwhelming to move toward the person we hope to become and the life we want to have.

As I stood surrounded by the damage of a disastrous fire, my bed-and-breakfast plan having literally gone up in smoke, I thought, *It can't get any worse than this.* I rely heavily on faith, but I also know that to change a bad situation, you have to use your inner strength.

Finding the inner strength to move out of any mess is a matter of examining the situation. *Just how bad is it?* I ask myself. If the answer is *This is bad, really bad*, then I know things can't get worse. If I'm this miserable and this sad, if

I've tried and tried and things don't feel like they will get better, if I feel like I can't win, then it makes good sense that any alternative to this awful situation will be better. It has to be.

In the middle of the fire damage, this understanding was enough to push me to make a different life choice, to find a way to overcome the present obstacle. This thought process of coaxing myself not to give up and to try a different path was not unfamiliar to me. I had understood this even as a young girl.

My mother left us when I was nine. "Your mother is not a good person," my dad often told us. "She's gone now. She doesn't exist anymore." These explanations made Brenda and me feel abandoned.

This was a pivotal life event, which required me to take on responsibilities not appropriate for my age. Although I did rise to the occasion, making sure that my little sister and I would survive, I also secretly cried into my pillow every night. Was it always going to be like this? Brenda and I came to believe that our mother would never return. But after six months, she did.

It was early morning and still dark when I heard the rustling beyond my bed. I opened my eyes to see the shadow of my mother hastily removing clothes from our bedroom dresser. What was she doing here? Here was our mother, the woman who Dad said didn't exist for us anymore, rifling through our things, grabbing what she could get her hands on, in a chaotic rush. At first, I kept still, motionless. I was afraid of her.

"Get your stuff," Mom ordered Brenda and me as we sat upright in our beds, shocked and stunned.

"Why?" Brenda asked her.

"We're leaving now!"

"No." Brenda began to cry. "No."

"We can't do that," I spoke up.

"Get moving," Mom said again, ignoring me. She was pressed and insistent. "You're coming with me now."

What did she mean we were leaving now? Why had she crept into our dark room making demands? My chest tightened with fear. I felt a fever-like burning rise to my cheeks and neck. My stomach knotted and my breathing became quick and shallow.

My mother must not have anticipated our worried and panicked reaction, because she stopped for a moment. She must have seen that her daughters doubted her plan. With little time to spare, she began to calm us as only a mother can, cooing at us. "You girls are everything for me. I've come back for you now."

She motioned for each of us to gather in her lap. "You belong with me," she said, giving me a kiss on the head and wiping a wayward bit of hair off Brenda's face. "I love you. You know that I love you, don't you?" she questioned. We nodded our heads in agreement.

There wasn't time to linger in this cuddly reunion or for

any further explanations. Our mother was on a time-sensitive mission.

"Let's go," she said again, with even more force now, and she resumed the haphazard packing. "Let's get moving."

Dad was already at the bakery, so this was an opportune time for her to take us without a fight. We worked quickly, wrapping up underwear, T-shirts, pants, a pretty red dress, and a few favorite toys in the frayed sheets and pillowcases ripped from our beds.

"Only take what you need," Mom directed us.

"Can't we bring everything?" I pleaded.

"No," Mom ordered. "Grab what you can and get in the car. We've got to move fast!"

We stuffed our belongings into the car and were ready to make our escape, still ignorant of where our mother was taking us, when I realized that one very important item was still missing: my dog, Tippy.

"Come on, Tippy," I called, making my way back to the house. "Come on!"

Mom gave me "the look" and sternly said, "That *dog* is *not* coming with us."

As much as I loved my mother, as much as I had wished for her return, I was not going anywhere without Tippy. This was not something I had to consider; it was an instant decision that was made in my heart. I stood my ground on our front walk, refusing to budge another inch. If my mother wanted me and Brenda to drive off with her, she would need to take Tippy too. We three were a package deal.

I looked Mom in the eyes and answered her in a voice as stern and insistent as her own. "I won't abandon Tippy. I'm not leaving Tippy like you left me and Brenda. If Tippy stays, then I stay!"

My mother's face puckered from the strain of frustration, anxiety, and hurry. We needed to escape before Dad returned home, and since his hours were unpredictable that could be at any moment. She was perspiring and I now saw deep creases near her eyes that I had never noticed before.

She had no choice. "Oh, all right," she caved. "Bring the damn dog."

I ran back inside the house to retrieve our curly-haired canine; when I returned to the car, Brenda had wiggled into a spot on the backseat among our disheveled belongings and Mom was poised behind the wheel. Tippy and I hopped into the front seat. As my mother pulled away from the curb, the morning light had just begun to splash over our big Snob Hill house. I could feel my heart thumping as I held Tippy tight in my lap, having no idea what the future would bring.

Much to my surprise, our new life with our mother was not so different from the last six months with our father.

My mother had left us to get herself established. "I've been getting things in order," she said, explaining the reasons for her long absence as we drove along. "So you would have a place to come to. So you would have a home."

Getting established meant this: My mother had purchased a hair salon in Prince Albert, which was twenty-five miles away. And now, instead of the big spacious house in an affluent neighborhood, we were to live in a small duplex by the train tracks—the wrong side of the tracks, by the way, complete with windows rattling when the trains rumbled by.

My mother, perhaps in an attempt to create a family for me and Brenda, pushed her live-in boyfriend into the picture. "He's your father now," she told us.

Our new "father's" name was Albert. He was a security guard at the Saskatchewan Penitentiary in the maximum-security unit. He was about a year younger than my mother, not even thirty. Albert was handsome, had a sports car, and liked to party. Today, I realize that he must have loved my mother a great deal to take on two young girls and a dog. But even if I had understood that at the time, I doubt it would have made me like the situation any better. I hated it.

One thing I knew for sure—if I ever got married, I would not make the same mistakes as my mother.

Eventually, Albert did become our legal stepfather. He was a rather quiet and somber man when sober, but there was something slightly rough about him. Aggressive. He was filled with frustration, and that festering anger turned to rage when he drank. He drank Thursday through Sunday nights.

It would start off with a casual drink as he tried to forget about the prisoners he faced every day at work, and about the responsibility he had for the young family he came home to every night. It was always the same routine. A drink, another drink, which led to some yelling, another drink, which led to screaming and nasty words, which led to hitting and choking my mother.

"I'm sorry, that won't happen again," Albert would promise us in the morning. "I don't remember what happened," he would say, and then he would cry. "I love your mother. I'm sorry. I love you guys too."

My mother also made her apologies. "Your father works so hard," she tried to justify. "Being a security guard in a place like that is unpleasant and dangerous. I can't begin to understand being around those sorts day in and day out, and you wouldn't want to imagine what crimes these inmates have committed to get themselves locked up," she told us. "But your father will do better now. I'll do better." Brenda and I would nod our heads, and for a time we were hopeful. After a while, we no longer believed him or her.

There were many incidents, all starting the same, all ending the same. Finally, my mother and stepfather came up with a new solution. We would move.

"We'll get a fresh start," my mother told us. "A clean slate should help," and I think my mother did believe that moving across the country would give them a chance to begin again. But I have since learned that making a change in location only relocates the problem.

We moved to Abbotsford, British Columbia, when I was

fifteen. I was unwillingly uprooted—ripped from my high school life and my boyfriend. To make matters worse, our new home was small, a two-bedroom apartment. Brenda and I shared a room and I slept on a piece of foam on the floor.

An unexpected phone call brought even more troublesome news. Albert had a daughter from a previous marriage, but he had not known her, had not been involved in her life or upbringing. Now, he learned that his child's mother was dead and Albert was her guardian. So another nine-year-old, exactly Brenda's age, joined us in the tight quarters, the three of us sleeping in one room. No one was comfortable with the new arrangement.

And the long-distance migration had not solved my mother and Albert's issues with each other. One weekend things went too far. They had gotten into it again, and my stepfather had my mother pinned up against their bedroom wall. As a pen guard, he was used to dealing with inmates; he was tough and rough. I threw myself into the middle of the brawl, trying to pull my stepfather off my mother, trying to keep my mother from receiving his blows.

I knew that Albert would not harm me. There was never any hostility aimed at us girls. My mother would take a beating, but if anything were to come her daughters' way, she would have become a mama bear. She would have stopped it. That was where she drew the line.

Finally, my stepfather, spent from the alcohol and physical exertion, stopped. He stormed out of the bedroom and into the living room, where he passed out cold on the sofa, leaving my injured mother to sink down the side of the wall, slumped and defeated. She had two black eyes, a bleeding nose, and there was a cut on her cheek. My mother and Brenda were crying. We were all terrified. I ran to get ice and facecloths.

I felt a murderous anger. I hated what he was doing to my mother. I hated her for letting it happen. Over and over. *This had to stop.*

I went into the living room, where my stepfather lay passed out on the sofa, removing himself from the unspeakable anguish he had caused. *This had to stop. Would he kill her next time? This had to stop.* It was then that I knew what to do.

I methodically disconnected the speaker wires from his heavy, dome-shaped stereo. Once the record-player base was free, I tugged to remove it from the shelf. This was a heavy piece of equipment and I could barely lift it, but the adrenaline coursing through my veins helped me carry it over to where my stepfather slept, unprotected and alone. I raised the black unit in the air over my head, positioning my weapon, and intended to bring my arms down with a swift, even blow to his skull. I was going to smash the hell out of him. Enough was enough.

"Don't!" my mother yelled in that tiny instant. "Don't!"

My mother took the stereo from me. I did not fight her. I knew she was right; harming my stepfather probably would not help matters one bit. It might even make things worse for my mother. But I now knew what blind rage felt like, and what it might make any of us do when we were pushed to the brink.

This fight must have been rock bottom for both my mother and my stepfather. "We can join AA or you can leave this house!" was my mother's ultimatum to Albert in the morning. They decided to try once more to change their lives. They joined Alcoholics Anonymous the next day. But I had been through enough and had little faith that anything would change. Shortly after, I decided to move out.

I graduated from high school in June and was living on my own by July 1. I knew I would never return to my parents' home under any circumstances. There had been no money for my college, no money to help me move out on my own, but I was not afraid to work. I knew I had to be self-reliant.

I was seventeen. I managed to get by on about $400 a month. My apartment rent was $200, and for $75 a month I rented furniture. I got around by bicycle as much as possible. My other expenses were a phone bill and food. I lived on canned kernel corn.

I was only barely getting by, but it turned out that the toughest part was not living on my own or supporting myself. It was leaving my little sister behind.

When my mother and Brenda would visit me, I pretended that I was doing better than I was, that it was cool to be on my own.

"Are you okay?" Brenda quizzed me.

"Why wouldn't I be?" I'd answer. "It's great. A lot of fun."

"Can I stay with you?" Brenda would beg.

"Not just yet," I'd tell her. "I'm so busy these days with work and all."

The truth was that I still longed for the security of being cared for. But I refused to let on that like Brenda, I, too, still needed a mother.

My early jobs consisted of everything from waitressing and hostessing in restaurants to working for a chiropractor to being a receptionist for a law firm. But there was one particular job that gave me a solid foundation for all that followed. And that job was one I actually started in high school: I sold vacuum cleaners.

I knew early on that I would need to work. I saw an ad in the local newspaper offering employment and the promise of good pay. I dialed the number. The man was a little vague about the job on the phone, but he asked me to come in the next morning for an interview.

When I got to the address, I saw that it was the dealership for Filter Queen vacuum cleaners. I found myself in a room with a peppy sales manager and a handful of other unemployed hopefuls who, like me, had answered the ad looking for a steady income.

"This job is door-to-door selling," the zealous sales manager explained to us. "You'll work for commission." At that point, one wormy middle-aged man and a frazzled woman in a pink tent dress got up and walked out. Three of us remained.

It was clear that the dedicated sales manager, Mr. Tim

O'Ryan, believed in the product. He caressed the round body of a silver metallic canister as he filled us in on the Filter Queen company—about attachments, hoses, and wands. Mr. O'Ryan demonstrated how the Majestic 360 sucked up all kinds of dirt and debris with a quick whoosh; he looked on with the admiration of a proud parent witnessing his firstborn performing an extraordinary feat.

Mr. O'Ryan's enthusiasm never wavered, his polished passion sustained through his closing lines. "Our products are classic," he said as if he were reaching the finale of an orchestral triumph. "Yes, these vacuum cleaners are more expensive than most. But you get what you pay for. Filter Queen's products are true quality, with high suction, incredible filtering, and extreme durability. When you purchase a Filter Queen, it's a product that stands by you for life. And that is not just good value, that is *great value* for the customer, and it means a high commission for you."

The three of us who had remained clapped, and Mr. O'Ryan gave a quick half-bow. He seemed quite pleased with himself and with his small audience. All three of us were hired.

"You can ride along with me," Mr. O'Ryan told me. "I'll give you half the commission from any sales that I make."

We knocked on twenty-two doors that day. Half of our would-be customers never answered the door, but we got two sales. I listened and learned from Mr. O'Ryan. And I realized that I could get by on one sale per day. It wouldn't be a great living, sure, but enough to live on. Of course, I hoped for much more than that someday. For now, it was what I needed.

On my first day out alone, I was anxious but also excited. Everything depended on me, rested on my shoulders. Another new hire was working one side of the ritzy neighborhood street. I canvassed the other side of the block. I knocked and knocked again. Door by door. If no one answered, I left my calling card. I didn't sell any machines that day. But the next day, a woman asked me to come back after supper. Well, it was a chance.

I had some pluses going for me. For one thing, it was mostly women who answered the front door, so as a young, energetic woman, it was easier for me to gain entrance than some of the guys working the neighborhoods.

My goals and expectations were simple: Sell as many vacuum cleaners as you possibly can. Some of the women who opened their doors did their own housework, others had maids. But this didn't matter much, because I learned that people didn't care how knowledgeable I was about vacuum cleaners. Women only cared that I cared. To survive, I needed to listen carefully to the customer, to figure out her concerns, and I used all of this when trying to make a sale. Years later, this same lesson became very helpful when I was growing my bed-and-breakfast business.

I also discovered that I had a talent for setting up home appointments. If I called a home during the day, usually a woman picked up the phone.

"Congratulations, Mrs. Brody, you've won a prize," I'd tell

her. "You can get one room of your house cleaned for free." It was an offer that most women didn't refuse. Later, while I was cleaning up the chosen room, I would boast about the great Filter Queen vacuum cleaner that I was using to make her room spick-and-span—point out how quick and easy it was to use. This got the customer's interest.

On the phone with cold calls, with just my youthful voice and my wits, I had to overcome the customer's reluctance and suspicions. If there was any trick to it, it all came down to not accepting that first no and getting the customer to keep talking. It meant listening—really, really listening to what she had to say. Was she too busy? Was her husband sick? Was she saddled with five children under the age of ten? If you could get someone talking about their concerns, their complaints, their daily difficulties, you could build a relationship and show them how a terrific product like Filter Queen would make a difference in their lives. You could convince them that they needed a good vacuum cleaner with all the bells and whistles—even if they didn't know it yet.

And that is exactly what I did. I believed in Filter Queen, and more importantly, I believed in myself. No was simply an obstacle to overcome. It was my job to puzzle over the problem, figure out how to get past the roadblock. I grew to love the challenge, to find my way to yes. That meant I had to find the connection between me and the lady of the house, even if the woman was twice my age. I paid attention. Was there a pet? A photograph of a child? Were the draperies heavy and easier to clean with a long attachment? It was all about getting the prospective client to trust me like a friend.

"This vacuum is a big purchase," a woman might balk. "It's just not in my budget."

"I understand," I'd counter, nodding my head to acknowledge her concern. "But I've noticed how dirty the entryway rug gets, and I've also noticed that you are a woman who takes pride in your home. I know you have to consider your budget. Most of us do. But I can work with you." I was sincere. I meant every word I said, and my customers felt that. It made all the difference.

In a short time, I was the top salesperson in my area.

Another bright spot during those days was Larry. I had met him in my senior year of high school and we clicked. He was one year older and so incredibly handsome. At first, we became friends. I thought Larry would be a perfect boyfriend. He was in college. He had a car. Since I couldn't ride everywhere on my bicycle, my only means of transportation, Larry would generously drive me where I needed to go. He also shared his family with me. A real family. One that pulled together and got along. Soon we became more than friends. At seventeen and eighteen years old, we fell in love.

I didn't have the chance to go to college right out of high school like Larry had done. I hoped that one day I could make my way there, but I was also getting a valuable education on my own. In a sense, I traveled many miles from door

to door, learning what made each woman tick, figuring out
how I might help make her life, and my own, a little better.

EXERCISES

Describe a recent time when you've felt totally alone, left
out, or even abandoned. What were two or three ways that
a positive perspective would have made all the difference?

_____

_____

_____

_____

An example:

> "I only had one can of kernel corn, but I decided to show my mother
> that my younger sister and I were just fine and had more than enough
> to eat for that day."

Regardless of how difficult a situation may be, a positive
outlook is critical for making a positive change. List one
attitude change that you know turned "nothing into something." This is called a "Why not?" moment!

CHAPTER 3

SETTING GOALS

If there was one thing I learned from selling vacuum cleaners, it was how to build a relationship with a customer. That's what I brought with me when I started selling cosmetics for Mary Kay.

Mary Kay beauty products are sold by independent "beauty consultants," and those consultants deliver the products directly to the customer's home or office. It was an opportunity to be my own boss without having to worry about a business license, insurance, product development, or branding. The Mary Kay company provided all that. It was an ideal and inexpensive small-business start-up.

I did need $750 for inventory at the start, which was a lot of money in the 1980s. You had to first buy the merchandise, then turn around and sell directly to customers. You had to have the inventory to make the sale. With my strong work ethic, sales experience, and a never-say-die attitude, I knew I could make this work, so I used my credit card to buy the products, and suddenly, I was a Mary Kay representative. More importantly, I was a business owner at twenty-two years old.

This is how it worked: If I bought a liquid foundation for $10, I sold it for $20 and made a 50 percent commission. But now I had the responsibility of being both boss and salesperson, so if I spent that $10 profit without buying more inventory, I wouldn't have anything new to sell. At first, when I started to see my sales grow, I thought, *Wow! I'm making all this money!* I immediately wanted to pay off all my bills and buy little extravagances. I learned the hard way that I couldn't spend all the money I collected from sales. I discovered pretty quickly that I had to plan ahead, control my cash flow, pay expenses, and then put money back into the business by restocking the product. I had to replenish my inventory.

Mary Kay taught me self-accountability. I didn't have an office, except in my home, and if I didn't sell anything, I didn't have a boss to push me or give me the "I'm very disappointed in you" speech. I had a Mary Kay director—sort of a cross between a mentor and a team leader—but she lived over an hour away. There were motivational and sales meetings, but they were all in Vancouver and too far away to attend. It was up to me.

Everywhere I went—grocery stores, beauty shops, the mall—I handed out my cards, offering free facials. "Have you ever heard of Mary Kay?" I'd ask. "I'm so excited to show you the products." And just as I had been at Filter Queen, I *was* excited. I'd sweeten the pot sometimes. "You know what," I'd say, "to make it more fun, invite your friends. I'll give them free facials too." The facials gave me the chance to show off the full cosmetics line. Business started off slow, but I kept trying and trying, meeting as many people as I could, telling them what I had to offer. Pretty soon one facial party became two, then three, and then I was doing five per week.

In sales, it's important not to make snap judgments about who will and won't buy. I'll always remember how I learned never to write off a sale. In the early days, I had an appointment in a neighborhood where mostly Vietnamese families lived, and from the look of the neighborhood, I made some pretty broad assumptions. *Oh, these people don't have any money to spend on cosmetics*, I thought. *I'm wasting my time here.*

I made the decision to cut my presentation in half. I only brought a limited amount of inventory into the house, leaving the rest in my trunk. What was the point? There would be no sales here.

The Vietnamese ladies who had gathered for the demonstration looked disappointed when I finished. They had expected more of a makeover, but everyone was kind and they helped me carry my products back out to my car. When I opened the trunk, they all gasped with delight. My trunk was full of eye shadows, perfumes, and lipsticks—all the things I had assumed they wouldn't want.

Boy, was I wrong! These ladies started grabbing everything. They wanted to see this lipstick, that eye shadow; they wanted to smell all the perfumes. I went back inside the house, hauling every one of my Mary Kay products like it was a Black Friday sale. I finished the presentation, which I had cut short. In a shopping frenzy, the women were ripping open the eye pencils and trying out the eye shadows. I panicked, even at that point, because I still assumed they didn't have the money to pay for all the things they were opening.

I regained control of the situation. I placed my products neatly across the table in the corner and started writing up orders in an organized manner. "What do you want?" I'd ask one, and I wrote it down. Then another: "What can I get for you?"

These women who I didn't think would buy *anything* cleaned me out. I came home with *twelve* one-hundred-dollar bills. Wow! I was on top of the world! I fanned those babies out: Who knew you could come home with this much cash legally?

The structure of the Mary Kay company gave me the opportunity to set broader, higher goals. The company is based on a reward system and makes a point of recognizing you for your work. This is a great feeling. At each level there are incentives: everything from a pearl necklace to getting to drive a pink Cadillac. This positive reinforcement was new to me. I thrived on it; I loved the challenge.

I realized there was both money and opportunity in

management; in fact, it was the only way to advance in the company's hierarchy. If I recruited three people, I got a percentage of whatever they made, plus free gifts and bonuses. Here was a way to step up my goals, and to earn more by shifting my focus from selling products to recruiting representatives. My sales technique was to recruit women at grocery stores and the mall.

Soon I was a team leader with lots of sales reps under me, and I was the one setting the pace. I gave my "girls" pep talks: "Come on! If I can do it, you can do it! Let's be the best team there is." And we were! I started getting thrifty. I turned the spare bedroom in the apartment I lived in with Larry into a place where I could do facials and product demonstrations. I arranged to have customers pick up their own orders rather than driving all around town delivering boxes door to door. I learned to work smart.

The momentum built. I had eight people on my team and had caught the attention of my director. If I moved up, she moved up, so she became very interested in working with me. Meanwhile I was always thinking, "I want to reach the next level. I want to be a senior director. I am going to drive the Cadillac."

When Mary Kay Ash founded the company, she intended to offer hope to women who lacked opportunity and financial support. She wanted to give them a means to become financially independent and transform their lives. Since an important part of my job was to show the women on my team how they could flourish, I needed to be a motivator too. My success depended on theirs. So, just as I had listened to my customers, I listened carefully to the women I was directing. Some of the women were not cut out for it and quit. Many got to a certain level where they felt comfortable and did not progress after that.

I saw lots of women who had low self-esteem and were running as fast as they could just to stay in the same place. These women needed something they could easily do that enabled them to take control of their finances and happiness. By recruiting them, I was filling that need. I was offering a chance to become an independent businessperson. I taught them how to build their business from the ground up, just as I had. I mentored them by going to banks with them to set up accounts. I taught them how to balance a checkbook. I taught them how to sell. I showed each of my team members how to use her individual knowledge and personal skills to make our customers feel beautiful and better about their appearance. I pushed them out of their comfort zones. Those Mary Kay representatives made good money for themselves—and for me.

I worked tirelessly. The challenges never stopped, because I kept moving up from team leader to director to senior director. After just thirteen months at Mary Kay, I earned my pink Cadillac! For me, it became all about how I could motivate and empower women. How I could break records and have my team grow with me.

One of the highlights of that time was the chance to fly to Dallas with my director to the Mary Kay National Convention.

I had to pay for my own airfare, but it was worth it. It was a wonderful event. I attended workshops and seminars on how to lead a team and how to get sales. All of this reinforced what I was doing—what I'd known intuitively how to do since my Filter Queen days. I felt so cool to belong to such an elite group, to be recognized for my skills and accomplishments. How amazing was this? Here I was, a young girl from the Canadian Prairies, sitting in a room full of established and savvy leaders. And now I was one of them.

After two years of being a senior director, the pressure of keeping my unit sales up, keeping myself and my team motivated, and the routine of weekly sales meetings started to be too much. I was working seventy to eighty hours per week. I was pushing myself too hard. I was exhausted, but more importantly, I felt like I didn't control my own life.

My experience with the company had taught me a lot. In a way, it was Mary Kay who made me the businessperson I am today. I was good at sales, but I learned management, discipline, and self-accountability (plus important things like managing income and expenses, sales volume, financial projections, branding, and marketing).

When I talk about *self-accountability*, this is what I mean: Set high goals for *yourself* and then never make excuses. If you don't succeed with your day's goal, don't cut yourself any slack. Don't say, "Oh, I guess that's not meant to be." Try harder the next time and keep trying until you do meet your goal, whether it's in sales, school, business, or even your personal life.

During my time with Mary Kay, many of the women I worked with were in situations similar to mine. Like me, some were selling Mary Kay because they didn't have an education and nobody was offering them a high-paying job, or because they came from a disadvantaged background. But often, these women didn't have the self-confidence or determination to find their way out of a going-nowhere life. They had defeatist attitudes. They were stuck. And when life got tough, they gave up too quickly.

I did understand the fear, heartbreak, and hopelessness felt in the face of unhappiness, when the stresses of marriage and the responsibilities of rearing children became overwhelming. I wanted to show these women how to take it a day at a time, an hour at a time, even minute by minute when necessary. Because you *can* find hope. You *can* take one baby step. You *can* make a plan to achieve. Use your fear as a great motivator. You don't have to stay running in place.

I'd started out wanting to make a better life for Larry and me (who was now my husband) and to provide for our future. I'd worked hard while he was continuing his education because I believed it was an investment in our life together. But now, I had to admit the truth—I was exhausted. Completely exhausted. It was time to take my own advice, to hold myself accountable to a new goal. I needed to find a stable and secure financial opportunity (something that Mary Kay was not and never would be). I needed to take control and put my life in balance. So, building on my efforts and the lessons I had learned at Mary Kay, I decided it was time to move on. And I did.

Do you need to move on in your life? Are you running in place? If you really look, there are probably many opportunities staring you right in the face. Opportunities where you might discover what you're good at, what your special talents are, what makes you happy and fulfilled—what will make you financially secure and independent.

Do you need to set higher goals or different goals? What action will you take?

EXERCISES

Self-accountability: This means to set high goals for *yourself* and not make excuses like "Oh, I guess that's not meant to be." The idea is to try, try again, and then try harder. This DOES NOT mean to keep doing things you know won't work. That will drive you nuts! But do keep trying and YOU WILL find something that makes a positive difference. Hold yourself accountable and never, never give up!

List two things you can do now that will help you hold yourself accountable.

1. _____

   _____

2. _____

   _____

An example:

"Today, I will hold myself accountable by sharing my afternoon goals with my best friend. I'm expect nothing from her/him except to listen about what I plan to accomplish."

Note: Writing down or sharing what you plan to do with someone you trust is a habit that dramatically increases real-time and positive change.

CHAPTER 4

KEEP THE BLINDERS ON

I left Mary Kay and an unstable financial life behind. I found a job with a government agency. For once, I had reasonable hours and a reliable paycheck. The agency distributed grants to companies that hired women in professions that were traditionally closed to women—work as welders, mechanics, and butchers. I loved the job.

And there was more good news. Things were going better for my mom and my stepfather. Joining AA had made a difference. They weren't fighting, had joined a church, and had invested in a small house. My stepfather had quit smoking. The physical abuse against my mother had stopped. He was sober.

But here's the thing about life sometimes: Just when you're getting comfortable, moving down the road toward your goals, a new and unexpected obstacle can tumble down in front of you, blocking your course. That's what happened to me.

Bam! I was laid off!

If you've ever been let go from a job, you know that it feels lousy and can rock you and your self-worth to the core.

In my case, the agency I was working for had started me out in marketing and I had worked my way up to handling contracts, assessing the qualifications of companies that applied for the grants. All was going well. Maybe too well, because my performance began to get noticed. All of a sudden, it became a concern that I was doing my job without a college degree. It didn't matter that I had been more than competent for over two years. I didn't have the degree. I was out.

Something I say a lot (especially when my goal seems a long way off and the path is full of obstacles) is "Keep the blinders on." What I mean by that is never get distracted or discouraged. Get your target in your sights and don't let anything stop you from achieving it.

Look at the way a champion racehorse bolts from the starting gate. Right from the start, the horse is intently focused on one thing: the finish line. Concentration on the end goal is as important as the speed of the winning horse. Other horses may jostle it, push and shove it, but the champion with its blinders on stays focused straight ahead. The jockey, too, has only one goal. No matter how difficult the track or the competition, horse and rider move forward together; nothing else matters.

Maybe the horse will win. Maybe not. But focus and concentration bring the pair closer to success. Keeping the blinders on, not getting distracted by what others are doing, concentrating on the goal: That's how you cross the finish line.

And so, like a good racehorse, I did not let getting laid off stop me. I found another good job in a doctor's office. And again, life was good. Larry and I seemed to be in a good place. After six years of irregular substitute teaching, Larry finally got a full-time job teaching elementary school. We were so excited. We were both working full-time, money was coming in. *All the hard work has paid off*, I thought. *This is how it's supposed to be! We are getting ahead!*

Larry and I had waited several years, and now we agreed it was the right time to start a family. Surprise! We were pregnant after only one month of trying. Nine months later we welcomed our daughter Carmen. Since the cost of a daily babysitter didn't make financial sense, I left my job to do some part-time work at home. So, within months, we were pretty much back to one income again.

My goals have always been to have a strong and enduring marriage, a happy and healthy family, and financial security—something I did not have as a child. But it can be hard to concentrate and focus on your goal. Especially when the journey toward your goal is far more difficult than you ever expected. If you stumble and lose your focus, join the club.

Like many women—and men, too, I suppose—I lost myself when I fell in love. I put myself last while focusing on strengthening my marriage. I didn't want to repeat the hurt that came from my parents' divorce.

Larry had set his sights on becoming a professor of English literature and had studied for years. I often helped him with his school papers: I'd go to the library to help with research; I'd stay up until 3:00 a.m. typing his papers. Sometimes I was so tired, I'd even type off the page. But I was happy to help him. We were married. *I'm doing this for us*, I told myself.

When Carmen was six months old, and I was twenty-eight, I decided to go back to school. I was only able to manage one psychology course, but I thought, *This is my start.* I didn't ever want to lose a job again because I lacked a college degree.

"I want to be a psychologist," I told Larry. "I want to help people."

Larry didn't embrace the idea. I noticed that he'd begun to show a negative streak about anything that might interest me. "What's the point in that?" he'd say. Or if we had visited with my friends on a night out, he'd remark later, "What a miserable time that was."

Despite the fact that we now had a baby (and then two, when Caitlin arrived four years after Carmen) and only one paycheck with plenty of expenses, Larry didn't want to follow a budget. He still wanted to travel, to enjoy an expensive bottle of wine, to go out to eat frequently. He didn't want to give up any of the extras of our former lifestyle.

I worked hard to keep him happy and calm, and to keep

the creditors away. If I didn't, he would begin to rant. "Are you kidding me?" he'd demand of me. "We can't get a bottle of wine?" And although I knew we couldn't afford it, that we should be tightening our belts, I'd feel that I had to buy it for him. I'd have to make sure that he had that drink, or that movie, or that fancy meal out.

"I'm trusting you to manage our money," he'd say. "Can't you even do that one thing right?"

"We have other bills," I'd try to explain. "We can't afford it. I'm having trouble paying all the bills." But in Larry's book that was no excuse. It was my fault.

"It's about managing and organizing properly," he'd lecture me.

"How long does it need to take to get out of the house?" he would scold me, as I tried to round up the girls and all of the things necessary for an outing. "Come on, it can't be that difficult."

I would try to anticipate Larry's concerns so that he wouldn't get annoyed at the girls or me. I walked on eggshells. Larry never got violent—he never hit like my stepfather had done to my mother—but I felt beaten down just the same.

I'd stand in our bedroom corner, my arms folded across my chest, while Larry shouted out my failings one by one. I was worthless. I wasn't smart. I wasn't educated. I couldn't even keep our finances in order. "You're right," I'd repeat over and over. "Yes, that's true. I'm sorry."

Larry never let me forget his superior education,

assuming that he, the educated one, naturally had more valuable insights and opinions than I did. To him, no matter what I achieved, I remained that "ignorant girl from the prairie." My opinion was certainly not worth much.

Outside the house, before I was a wife and a mother, I was recognized as a competent problem-solver in all of my jobs, but at home I was browbeaten and full of self-doubt. How had I arrived in this spot?

I married young and allowed my plans to hinge upon the desires of my husband. Those always took first priority. Some of that was because it was customary at the time, and some of it was because I thought that when you got married you automatically adopted the same goals as your husband. Most of all, I had a vision of having the best and longest marriage on record. Unlike my parents, there would be no divorce for me. I could endure a few hiccups.

I don't think I was unusual in my thinking. A lot of women are fixated on keeping their marriage going at any cost. They don't bother to see how little they are being cared for, how the marriage isn't a two-way street, how verbal abuse can beat them down. That's when it's necessary to get your bearings, to notice what might have changed around you. To notice if somewhere along the way you've become lost.

Just because I wanted our marriage to be great didn't make it so. Larry and I had both wanted kids, and two wonderful, beautiful daughters, Carmen and Caitlin, came into our lives. But as time went on, I turned out to be the one who spent the time and energy on them. Larry rarely could make the time. He did not show up for the events, large or small, in our daughters' lives. He thought birthday parties were just an occasion to drop by for a quick hello before he dashed off again.

I truly believed that Larry's education was the key to our family's well-being. I thought it meshed with *my* goals of security and freedom, a life far from the hunger that plagued my own childhood. What I didn't want to admit was that Larry was a professional student. His years of all-consuming study were not a quest for knowledge or a passion for lifelong learning; they were more of an avoidance of family involvement and responsibility.

"Just be patient for a bit more," Larry would assure me. "Things are going to be great." Change was always postponed until later.

As the years went by, Larry went to school for longer and longer hours, and I raised our two beautiful girls, which was rewarding, but also frustrating when I kept waiting for the "later" that never came. Ballet recitals, school plays, concerts, teacher conferences, doctor visits, and homework all received the same response: "I can't go. I'm studying." It got to the point where Larry's schooling was his whole life and left no room for anything or anyone else. Not his kids, not me. I was married but I was alone, and lonely.

I had to take a hard look at the honest truth—Larry kept me in line with disregard, insults, and put-downs. I allowed this for too long. Finally, I had had enough. I needed and wanted to find a way to be independent, financially and emotionally, from my husband. That was a turning point for me. Now I knew exactly what I needed—a new plan.

What do you need to see clearly and honestly? What direction is right for you now?

EXERCISES

You, too, may need to take a fresh look at yourself and your situation, whether that means a troubled marriage, a dead-end job, or an unsupportive relationship with a friend or family member. You may need to admit the truth about your circumstances.

List at least one major change you would like to see happen in the next month. Yes, in just one month. Every Monday–Friday for the next month, list three actions you can take that day that will help you make this change.

Three important things I will do today that will help me achieve my goals:

1. _____
2. _____
3. _____

Example:

"I want to feel better about myself regardless of any outside influence or circumstance."

1. Today I will only watch thirty minutes of television, because more than that depletes my emotional energy and distracts me from accomplishing my goals.

2. Today I will exercise (walk fast around the block) for at least twenty minutes. This gives me the strength to achieve my goals and helps my body rest and sleep at night.

3. Today I will call at least three new people and tell them about my new business. If positive change is going to happen, I have to keep the blinders on, not be distracted, and do something now!

Focus on these daily goals, and take note of whether you are on track to achieve them. Every day, reassess. Ask yourself, what are three things I will do today that will help me not be distracted and do whatever it takes to make change happen? If you do this every day, no matter what, for one month, watch out! Your life is already starting to change! Why not?

CHAPTER 5

THE MYTH OF BEING READY

The name of my bed-and-breakfast was Abbotsford Classic Bed & Breakfast. The business idea originally began as my exit plan—a way to make myself financially independent—and with two children, it was a way to earn a living from home. It would give me the means and confidence to leave my marriage, if and when that became necessary. But when the unthinkable happened and a fire swept through our house, leaving my plan in ruins before I'd even started, nearly everything was destroyed—including my spirit and determination.

This was one of the lowest points in my life. Here we were, Larry, me, and the girls, forced to live in a crowded, seedy hotel for three months as our house was *slowly* put back together.

And if that wasn't enough, life was full of fighting. Fighting with the insurance people. Fighting with the renovation guys (who, I found out, didn't even *have* insurance and weren't covered at all). Fighting to rid the house of lingering smoke. And I was fighting with Larry. He didn't let me forget that it was *my business idea* that had gotten us into this mess. It was a daily struggle just to get the house fixed and restored to how it had been before the fire, let alone to re-create from scratch the bed-and-breakfast I had envisioned.

I was tired. Dead tired. *How am I going to continue?* I kept asking myself. *How can I move ahead?* I wondered how I was supposed to raise my girls in a happy household when I didn't even have the money to feed them. We were broke. I had tried so hard and now everything that I had worked for was gone.

I'm done, I told myself. *I just can't do this anymore.* And that is where I found myself—emotionally spent and completely discouraged. I don't like to admit it, then or now, but I was ready to quit. Ready to give up on any more plans for a better future. It seemed easier to give in and accept what was, even though "what was" was pretty lousy.

This was still the state I was in when a soft-spoken little old lady called me a few weeks later, shortly after we'd moved back into our house. She wanted to stay in the bed-and-breakfast. "We're not open," I told her. "We've had a fire and we're not quite ready."

"I don't care about that," the woman said. "My husband is in the hospital here and I'm from out of town. I just don't want to stay in a hotel."

I didn't *feel* ready, and I guess the truth is that I wasn't ready; there was a lot left unfinished, but here was opportunity literally calling me on the phone. This agreeable woman needed a room and I needed to get my business going.

Well, why not? I thought. "Sure," I told her. "Let's do it."

And so, Shirley, a music teacher from the States, was my first official guest. She stayed for one month. I didn't pry into her personal life and she didn't pry into mine, but she was my guinea pig. Each day I got her something else she needed for her room. We made a joke of it.

"What do you need today?" I'd ask her. "What would you like?"

And Shirley would very politely tell me. "Oh, I need a toaster, dear," she'd say with her slightly nasal American accent, and I'd run out and get her a toaster. "It would be so nice to have a microwave," she'd mention. The next day, I'd buy a microwave. And the day after that, a teakettle. I'd leave fresh muffins and cereals in her room too. This is how I figured out what sorts of things a guest would want.

There is power in action, and taking care of Shirley's needs made me feel like I could get my bearings once again. I began to feel that I could actually make this bed-and-breakfast business happen. Imagine, I was at home with my kids and I was making some money. And having guests like Shirley for company was far easier than having Larry around. *Hmm, not bad*, I thought. *Maybe instead of just one room, I should have a few.* Thus the Abbotsford Classic Bed & Breakfast began (again) with three rooms to rent.

My life would never be the same.

The guests came and went through a separate entrance and so they never bothered Larry, not that he was home much anyway. There was the Roman Room and the Classic Room. I converted the garage into the Garden Room. Each space had a kitchenette. Later, I even divided up my family room to accommodate more guests. The Garden Room was extra-special, with a fireplace, a private bath, and lots of pretty white linens. It was romantic. I offered a Champagne Package, which included rose petals and chocolates. Of course, it was not lost on me that while I was busy organizing romantic weekends and even weddings for complete strangers, at night I was upstairs in my own bedroom alone and miserable.

If I still wasn't getting smart about the state of my marriage, I was getting very clever about my business. I found it was easier to rent by the month when I could, as this was lower maintenance. To help expand my marketing efforts, I reached out into the community and joined the Chamber of Commerce. I quickly became part of their Tourist Committee. When you put yourself out there, you meet people. And that's what I did.

Through my involvement with the Abbotsford Chamber of Commerce, I had the opportunity to do some marketing work for the Abbotsford Airport. I sold advertising on the airport's billboards to hotels and to WestJet airline. The Abbotsford Airport Authority, WestJet, and the Chamber of Commerce all liked my work. The next thing I knew, I was hired to help start a new tourism magazine to encourage people to come to the area. I remember one issue was intended to promote golf. It didn't matter that I knew nothing about golf. I had the guts to figure it out—to get into my car and drive one hour out to Rowena's, a fancy resort with the most prestigious golf course in the area. "If you buy an ad, I'll give you the front page of the magazine," I promised them. Rowena's bought $5,000 worth of ads! They were *definitely* on the front page.

Now, I was a thriving business owner and a subcontractor to the airport. If that's not proof that things can change, can turn around, I don't know what is. I'd taken what I'd learned about the hospitality business and put it together with what I knew about marketing, branding, and sales—all the things I'd learned from Filter Queen and Mary Kay. It worked!

I helped start five new adventure/travel/lifestyle magazines and I got commissions on all the advertising sales! Our success with the publications worried the British Columbia tourism board, and they eventually bought out all the magazines to keep them under their umbrella. They offered me a job too. I didn't take it, though; I preferred to be my own boss.

But here's the important thing in all this—one opportunity led to another. I didn't let doubt stick around for long. And I didn't let doubt keep me from trying, even if I knew nothing about golfing, or adventure tours, or whatever we were putting together for the current magazine.

Meanwhile, my bed-and-breakfast had grown to four bedrooms, which now classified it as an inn. My girls—who were eight and twelve around this time—estimated later that in the four or five years the inn was open, we had only seven nights without guests in our house.

I was busy, busy. I would get up in the morning and see to the guests, preparing and serving breakfast and making sure everyone was satisfied. I made beds, made sure the laundry was done, and then I'd run the kids to school, go to the airport, take care of my marketing jobs, go to Chamber of Commerce meetings, and sell, sell, sell. Then I'd come back, pick up the kids from school, check in new guests, and start all over.

I won't tell you that it wasn't a lot of work. It was. But I was my own boss and I was making $10,000 to $12,000 per month. I was doing pretty well for a "homemaker," don't you think?

Still, I kept trying to please Larry (without success). On one of my routine trips to the liquor store for a bottle of wine, I noticed a brochure promoting jet-boat excursions. The owner, a pretty blonde, was photographed standing next to her boat. She seemed to be running a small business that took people out on the Fraser River for guided fishing tours. The magnificent river, just outside Abbotsford, is only an hour or so from Vancouver, and tourists are willing to drive out for a side trip because the Fraser River has a huge number of migrating salmon. Since I was now looking for other kinds of experiences and adventures for my guests, I liked the sound of it. Maybe we could help each other out by sharing customers. I called the woman up.

"Before I recommend something to my guests," I told Ruthie, the owner, "I'd like to try it out myself." Ruthie was friendly and gracious. She immediately invited me onto her boat.

I accepted. Larry, who didn't know how to fish at all, decided for some reason that he wanted to come along. "You're not doing that alone," he told me.

Meeting Ruthie changed my life. We hit it off immediately. We clicked. Ruthie and Larry did not. Larry was miserable and did not enjoy one moment of the trip. Larry's behavior did not go unnoticed by Ruthie. She said a lot with her eyes, looking from him to me, catching my eye with a quizzical look.

"What's with your husband?" Ruthie asked me toward the end of the trip.

I didn't feel comfortable discussing it with her in that moment, especially as Larry was in earshot, so I politely said, "That's just him. This is not his thing." Ruthie seemed to understand.

"Do you think we could find a time and try this again?" Ruthie whispered to me. "Just the two of us?" I must have hesitated because Ruthie added, "Maybe when he's teaching during the week. Nobody will know."

About two weeks later, Ruthie did call. "I'm taking the boat out today," she said. "Can you come along?"

I agreed, and soon we were gliding along the scenic Fraser River.

We had a blast. It was one of the most memorable days I've ever had. Ruthie made lemonade and margaritas. She cut the engine and we free-floated down the river, laughing and sharing our stories. Ruthie was not unlike me.

Finally, she was comfortable enough to ask me again, "So, what's with your husband?"

"I'm so unhappy," I confessed to her without holding back, and it was a relief to tell someone who I thought might understand. "I've been unhappy for the last seven years of my marriage and I need to get out."

"Me, too!" Ruthie said.

"No way!" I exclaimed.

"Yeah," she said. "I've been married twenty-three years."

"Wow!" I blurted out. "So have I!"

Ruthie and I had a lot in common. We were both struggling. We both had small kids. I had two daughters and she had three. We were both trying to build our own businesses as a way to find independence from unhappy marriages. Our afternoon on the boat was the beginning of the best friendship—and we are good friends to this day. We have supported each other as we've moved along into new and independent lives.

When it is necessary to make a change in your life, I believe friends are important. And you don't need many. One or two good friends can offer huge support. Things seem a bit easier when you have someone to listen to you, who will empathize with your struggles and fears, who will help you get through.

Do you need to make yourself financially stable or independent? Would you like to try something new or leave a job that does not serve you? Is there a business you've always wanted to start? Or do you see a need in your community and have an idea of how to fill it? Even if you don't feel *ready* (who is ever completely ready?), can you find a small way to begin? What are the local organizations you might join to help you reach or expand that goal?

When you get out and about, all kinds of inspiration and opportunities appear. You'll find ways to get unstuck, and you'll meet new people—people who just might understand, people who might help you change your life.

EXERCISES

There is power in action, and helping someone who needs a helping hand, whether it be in business or personal life, keeps you from being the center of your own universe.

List one or two things you can do for someone today that are a random act of kindness. Remember, you're not doing this to prove anything or to impress anyone. Giving someone a simple gift or doing a simple action for someone "just because" causes your perspective and attitude to change. By doing something kind for someone else, you become open to new possibilities that something good will happen to you. Just do it!

Two random acts of kindness that I will do for someone today are:

1. _____

2. _____

CHAPTER 6

THE COURAGE
TO SAY YES

I bolted upright in bed. My heart raced. In my nightmare I'd been running—dragging my sister by the hand as we raced through a neighborhood of old and unfamiliar houses. I had no idea where I was. I had no idea where I was going. Brenda and I zigged and zagged, not wanting to find ourselves on a long street where our father's car might easily overtake us. We ran hard—as fast and as far as our small legs could carry us.

Moments after waking, I realized that I was not a child running but an adult in my own bed, perspiring and rattled. But it was more than just an awful nightmare or some scene out of a horror movie: It was a real-life memory from when I was ten years old.

The incident (which I will never be able to completely shake) was during the time after my mother had come to get us from our dad's house, and she had taken Brenda and me from Snob Hill to live with her and my future stepfather in Prince Albert.

My grandmother (on my mom's side) had traveled to Prince Albert to visit us and on that particular afternoon she came with Brenda to pick me up early from school. It was a surprise I hadn't expected. The principal came to my classroom and asked that I step into the hall. I was terrified. Had I done something wrong? I couldn't think of a thing, but I knew that when a principal pulled you out of your fourth-grade class it couldn't be good.

"Everything is okay," the principal reassured me. "Your grandmother is here. You'll be going home with her."

This was a great treat for me. I adored my grandmother. I only have a few fun childhood memories, and spending time with her on the farm where she lived with my grandfather are some of the best. I loved chasing the cattle in the fields. I loved to watch the hay being cut. I loved helping my grandmother prepare and deliver the meals to the cattle hands. We'd garden. She'd let me have morning coffee with her. Most of all, I cherished that my grandmother thought I was special. I didn't have to be a mom to Brenda when Grandma was around. I got to be a kid.

And so on this afternoon, I was in heaven. I assumed that since my mother was working, my grandmother had decided to come and walk me home. Grandma held Brenda's hand, and I skipped up alongside my grandmother, slipping my fingers into her other hand, the three of us making our way down the sidewalk.

We hadn't gotten very far when, without warning, a car zoomed up over the curb and stopped fast in front of us. My father jumped out from the driver's seat. I can't remember what he said or if he said anything that made sense. I just remember him gibbering nervously.

Dad grabbed Brenda first and tried to drag her into the backseat of his car. I was screaming while Grandma clung to Brenda's arm with all her strength and Dad pulled Brenda's other arm. It was a brutal tug-of-war.

Dad must not have expected such resistance. He shoved my frail and very short grandmother hard against the chain-link fence behind us. That shove caused my grandmother to let go of Brenda's hand and to slump against the fence. Surprised by his own violence, my dad stepped back and let go of Brenda's other arm. I knew what I had to do. Run! I had to run fast and far away. Now! It was up to me to protect us. I reached for Brenda's hand, which by this time must have been awfully sore, and we took off.

We ran through backyards, front yards, and alleys. We scrambled over parked cars. We had no idea where we were, but we kept running. We'd occasionally stop to catch our breath, hiding behind a shrub or a detached garage. For me, it was a matter of life and death.

I have no idea why I was drawn to the particular house where we went for help. Both Brenda and I were still crying and exhausted when I knocked on the wooden door. When the door swung open, I could not believe my eyes. Here stood a nun dressed in full religious habit, and for the first few moments all I saw was a contrasting blur of a snowy white wimple and the stark black garment draping to the ground. I knew who nuns were because I'd read the *Madeline* children's books. But I had never actually seen a real nun—especially up close.

I think the nun was as surprised to see us as we were to see her. Here we were, two panicked little girls, breathless and sobbing, standing on her porch. She puzzled over our presence but we could sense her kindness.

"Calm down," the nun told us. "It's going to be okay."

She had us step inside. It seems we had found ourselves in the nuns' living quarters of a Catholic school. There was a long hallway, which ran to a kitchen in back of the house where we could hear the clanging of pots and pans. The room to the left was a little chapel. It smelled like wax with a faint trace of incense. The nun took us to the room on the right. It was a small sitting room with a shabby old sofa and a couple of chairs that must have been hand-me-downs from a parishioner's dining room.

Once we were safely settled on the sofa, the nun put in a call to the police. They soon arrived and I felt panicky all over again. But as I began to tell them what had happened, my fear just melted away. In its place was a bit of anger, and also a kind of focused determination that I'd never felt before. I was learning how to calm myself in difficult and compromised circumstances. This determination made me very clear—I would always look out for myself and for my young sister. I also knew that although I didn't much care for my stepfather, I would never return to my father.

The police put us in the backseat of the patrol car as we searched the nearby streets for signs of my father and his car. We didn't find him, but we were reunited with my grandmother, who was dazed and worried as she frantically walked the neighborhood in search of us.

Years later, I learned that my father had been threatening my mother that day and she had sent my grandmother to fetch me early from school, to get me out of there. After that day, my father never bothered us again.

Now, as I tried to shake off my very real nightmare, that same feeling began to wash over me: a feeling of pure determination. It occurred to me that this dream wasn't some random memory that I happened to recall. The message was clear. It was once again time to run toward a safe haven. I needed to grasp my daughters' hands and run. I needed to protect them, too.

At that time, before the bed-and-breakfast expanded and I began making good money, I still had lots of unpaid bills and was asking myself lots of questions, like "How will I support my kids?" and "How will I be able to earn more to make it on my own?" I knew I was going to end up a single mom, and I was scared—really scared. If we were going to eat, if we were going to have a roof over our heads, then things had to change and change quickly. I refused to ever again be that baker's daughter without a crust of bread to eat.

It's probably no surprise that my relationship with Larry had grown worse. Right after the fire, he started working toward his doctorate in education, which required that he travel to San Diego every summer for study. I didn't like that he left every summer, but I was trying to hang in there, trying to be supportive.

"One day maybe we will even get to move to California," Larry told me.

That first summer actually seemed like it would be fun. Larry had rented a deluxe apartment in San Diego. It had a swimming pool and tennis courts. "I need a nice place to study," he said, justifying the money. He sweetened the deal by promising, "You and the kids can come out for the last week. It will be a family vacation for all of us."

The reality was that we couldn't afford this kind of luxury and his mom chipped in a lot. Our family vacation didn't go well. In fact, it was more like the vacation from hell. Larry didn't want us there. Since he was away in the summers and rarely at home during the year, he was no longer used to us being together as a family. He had his routine, and the kids and I weren't part of his schedule. We were cramping his style.

During one of our vacation fights, I asked him a question: "Tell me, if you had to do it all again, at the cost of your marriage and family, would you still go down this path to complete your education?"

He didn't miss a beat when he answered, "In a New York minute! My studies are my personal Mount Everest."

This gave me a big dose of reality. I immediately asked for a divorce.

I wasn't the only one suffering from my husband's actions; Carmen was suffering too. She was getting bullied and taunted at school because her father taught there. Every day for seven months Carmen came home teary-eyed and I could see that she was losing self-esteem. I thought it was best for her to change schools and was thinking of putting her in private school, but Larry wouldn't hear of it. "She'll toughen up," he said. And when I pushed, he became really annoyed. "Oh, that will look just great," he argued, using his best sarcastic tone. "How can I pull my kid out of the school where I teach and put her in private school? That makes perfect sense!"

But watching my daughter in such a miserable state was not acceptable to me, and for one of the first times in my marriage, I went against my husband's wishes. I enrolled both of my girls in a private Christian school that was known to be nurturing. Larry reacted to my rebellion by refusing to drive the girls to school or attend any of their school events. It made me feel even more like a single parent, but I knew I had done the right thing for my daughters.

Following Larry's return home from San Diego that

summer, I noticed he was even more impatient with me. It wasn't until the Christmas party at the school where he worked that I figured out why.

At the party, Larry and I were standing in a circle of his colleagues when a cute young teacher joined us with her husband.

"I want you to meet my partner," she said as she introduced Larry to her husband. Then she confidently turned to me and said, "I'm Larry's partner."

At this point I didn't know who she was other than a fellow teacher, but I thought I'd make a little joke, and I said, "Oh, that's funny; actually, I'm Larry's partner. He's my husband."

I guess my silly sense of humor was misunderstood, because both Larry and this young woman became visibly flustered. She began to fidget and turned red in the face. Larry seemed uncharacteristically nervous too.

Wait a minute! I thought. *What is this about?* I'd only been joking, but I had certainly stumbled onto something. I felt sick to my stomach, but I said nothing.

With my radar up, I started watching more closely. When Larry worked late (which was every day), saying he had to finish report cards or catch up on correcting homework or prepare the next day's lessons, I'd drive over to the school (long after the school had closed for the day) and there would be only two cars parked in the lot. Guess whom they belonged to? It gave new meaning to all those nights when Larry was "working late." Larry was having an affair.

His lover even came to our house unannounced on his

birthday once. She arrived at our front door holding a large bouquet of balloons with HAPPY BIRTHDAY written in bright colors.

"Is Larry here?"

"No," I answered, shocked that she would be brazen enough to show up at our door.

"Can you give these to Larry?" she asked me. "I wanted to wish him a happy birthday."

As the days and weeks went by, my rage mounted. Not only was Larry hard to live with, now he was also cheating on me!

The girls loved their dad, and in his own way, he loved them. But staying together and living in this kind of marriage wasn't going to happen anymore. It was not healthy for any of us. I'd waited a long time and now he had to go. To make things easier, to avoid all the unpleasant drama for the girls and me, I decided not to confront him and waited to make my move the following summer while he was in San Diego.

In the meantime, the husband of Larry's girlfriend found out about the affair. He made his wife quit her job. They moved to Florida and she became pregnant. Larry never told me any of this, and I had not yet confronted him about the affair, but he went into a major depression, which didn't help our home life one bit.

When summer finally arrived and it was time for Larry to leave for his studies in San Diego, I was more than ready. I packed as many of his clothes and belongings as I could fit into his car. He would be away all summer, but this time was different. It was an eerie and surreal day. This day was the last day of our marriage. We had lived twenty-three years together, but I alone knew that Larry was not coming back into our home. The girls didn't know, Larry didn't know, but I knew. I had no idea how or when we would divorce, but this day's good-bye was permanent.

As Larry drove away from the house, the girls waving, I breathed a sigh of relief. Throughout that summer, the girls and I would chat with him on the phone. At first, I pretended everything was normal, but the clock was ticking, and I knew I would not allow him to return. If I did, I would never have the strength to get him out.

Now here's the truth. I stayed in a bad marriage for years after I knew it was not good for any of us. That was partly due to the fact that I did not want to be divorced. I didn't want to follow the path of my parents and I desperately wanted a good and strong marriage. But mostly it was due to fear. It took me years to admit that my marriage was over, and then it took me years to take action. I went through all the stages of grief when I was still in the marriage—the loneliness, depression, resentment, anger, and, finally, acceptance. But I could not stay and accept the status quo. While I had been able to overcome numerous obstacles with business and finance, I had been slow to initiate change in my marriage. But now I thought, *It can't get any worse.*

If I were a different sort of person, I might have cried, but I was cried out. Or I might have blamed myself for allowing someone else to have so much control over me. But that wouldn't have served any purpose. The only thing I could do was to make a change. Right then.

Larry called one night and I told him my decision. "We argue all the time," I said. "We've fallen out of love, and you've had an affair."

Larry denied it all. When I didn't back down, he began pleading. "I promise to change. Just give me one more chance," he begged me.

After years of waiting, I was done with chances. "Coming back is not good for me, the girls, or anyone."

Since pleading hadn't worked, Larry began to demand. Maybe he expected that I would retreat to my old habits of low self-esteem and say something like "You're right. I know I've messed up," or "Yes, sir, I'll try harder." But I didn't. I held my own against his anger.

During part of that telephone argument, my oldest daughter, Carmen, then twelve years old, came into the room and stood close by me, listening. I kept repeating to Larry, "You can't come back!" And Larry kept saying, "I'm not leaving. I'm coming home."

Finally, after this had dragged on for a while, Carmen quietly handed me a piece of paper. On it she had boldly and wisely written, "Mom, you always know the right thing to do. Just do it!"

That's all I needed. She knew. I knew. My marriage to Larry was over. He was out and not coming back. There was nothing further to discuss. The conversation needed to end.

"No," I said to him firmly. "You are not welcome here." I hung up.

Years later, Larry's mistress called me. I guess her conscience got the best of her, because she wanted to apologize. I didn't have much to say to her, but I could honestly say one thing. "Thank you for the excuse to push forward," I told her. "I needed to get out."

If you're someone who is resolved to "do the right thing" but you feel afraid and stuck in a relationship, believe that you can do what seems impossible. If you're 100 percent committed, you can make that break from an emotionally or physically abusive relationship.

It's not easy to break the cycle, but you can do it! You should not and cannot stay in any relationship that has no future. That doesn't mean that marriage vows aren't important and that we shouldn't do everything possible to maintain a healthy relationship, but when it becomes clear that the relationship is detrimental, you should end it. As it turned out, my new friend Ruthie and I ended our marriages just six months apart. As I said, we leaned on each other for support.

I know all too well that overcoming fear is difficult. We've all been in fearful situations. Young or old, we all know what it's like to run from what frightens us most. When you find yourself running blindly from what you are afraid of, stop and ask yourself: *Can I overcome this problem? If I can't do it by myself, can I find someone to help?*

Start by having the courage to say yes.

Your fear can be a big influence. It can be the thing that spurs you on to save yourself and your family. There's always a choice to be made. Do you choose to continue running away? Or will you choose to stand your ground and believe that somehow, some way, everything will work out? Can you use the energy that comes from fear and put it toward positive, constructive action?

As the kind and knowing nun promised Brenda and me on that terrifying afternoon, "It's going to be okay."

EXERCISES

Name a relationship in which you found obstacles, anger, indifference, and harm, rather than happiness and support. This may have been with someone close to you, like a spouse, relative, or friend, or this relationship could have been with a casual acquaintance or coworker. Regardless of who, describe one or two things you did to sever the relationship.

_____

_____

_____

_____

When you were at your "wit's end" and you knew that continuing the relationship would only bring harm to yourself and others, what are at least two things you did to find courage for making the break?

1. _____

_____

_____

_____

2. _____

_____

_____

_____

How did doing these two things give you the courage to make the break?

CHAPTER 7

MAKING MEMORIES

"Why can't you have a boat?" Kenny pressed me. Kenny was the new man in my life and he wasn't the kind of guy who let words like "can't" or "impossible" stand in his way.

"Are you crazy?" I protested. "I *can't* just go out and buy a boat. Or has it slipped your mind that I'm a single mom with two daughters to take care of? Buying a boat would be dumb. Irresponsible."

Kenny did not give up easily. He knew my situation. We'd been dating for six months. He also knew that my bed-and-breakfast was thriving, that Carmen and Caitlin were well cared for, and that I had always longed for a boat.

"Is that so?" he challenged me with a big grin. "If a boat is going to make you happy, how is that going to hurt you or your kids?"

I'd never looked at my life, at my desires, that way before. I'd never thought I could entertain the idea of buying something *just for fun*. Something luxurious *just for me*. This kind of thinking was definitely outside the box.

While part of me still felt this idea was crazy, I could see that Kenny had a point: I'd dreamed of having a boat forever, but it wasn't a dream that I'd ever hoped to achieve. Now, the idea of owning a boat represented what I could do on my own. Kenny's questions made me realize that if I wanted to do it, I could accomplish this all by myself. It made me smile when I digested the fact that I was the one who could and would make this decision—not my ex-husband.

Kenny kept making his point. "What's the worst thing that could happen, Cathy?"

So I asked myself: "Could I lose money on a boat?" *Maybe, but I could remake money.* "Could I drown?" *I guess that was a possibility, but I could learn how to drive a boat, or take along somebody who knew what they were doing.* I continued quizzing myself and I started to feel like the worst thing that could happen was that I wouldn't go for it, that I wouldn't take the risk.

So I did it. I worked extra hard. I figured out a plan that made sense, and I found the courage to go and get a loan. It wasn't easy, but eventually I bought my boat.

Of all the choices in the boatyard, *Dream Maker* was the one for me. The name caught my attention right away, and it was painted across the wide flat transom in gorgeous blue letters for all to see. This thirty-eight-foot Fiberform motorboat had a bedroom in the forward bow and even had a little kitchen. (I would soon have to learn the nautical terms "cabin" and "galley," to go along with the boat!) It was built for ocean traveling and it could sleep six. I still didn't know much about boating and I'm not sure that Kenny really did either, but somehow we made our way out of the marina that afternoon and into the ocean.

That day changed my life.

There has always been something about the ocean that touches me deeply. I lived on the prairie as a child, and the first time I ever saw a photo of the ocean, I knew I wanted that in my life. I wanted to be near water. Ocean water.

After I met my friend Ruthie, I spent a good bit of time with her on the Fraser River. I liked being on her fishing boat, and I always loved any reason to be with her, but I never felt the emotional connection with the river that I do with the ocean. To tell you the truth, I was a little afraid of the river. The Fraser is narrow, the current fast, and the water cold. If you fall in, you could easily drown.

The Pacific Ocean, on the other hand, is open and wide and full of possibility, and the way in which the light hits the water makes the ocean look different every day. You never see the same thing.

When I bought *Dream Maker*, my bed-and-breakfast was going well and expanding, my girls and I were making our way without Larry, and Kenny was prodding me along, making me think about how my attitude toward life could be different and fun. Kenny was a big fan of spontaneity. This was the polar opposite of Larry, who was content to stay in the same house year after year. We would have died in that house. Our life together was about planning for the future and never enjoying the moment.

"We should live every day to the fullest," Kenny would say to me. "Let's make a memory." This was an approach to life I'd never experienced before. It made me nervous, but I was ready to try. Kenny was the perfect teacher.

Kenny was born sparkling and vibrant, and he wasn't just talk and no action; he did live life to the fullest. He worked in real estate, selling lots and home designs in housing developments. He wasn't wealthy, but he worked hard and was making more money than me, and he knew how to have fun. He worked hard at that, too.

It turned out that *Dream Maker* was about so much more than buying a boat. To me, it symbolized freedom for me and my girls; it was about stepping into a new life of possibility, and living in the moment instead of always putting fun on hold. Now, I had the ability to be on the water with my children and friends. We were making memories.

We moored *Dream Maker* in the seaside community of White Rock, about forty-five minutes away from Abbotsford. White Rock has a sandy beach and is located on the waters of Semiahmoo Bay. There is a long promenade and, as the name implies, a large white rock. Kenny and I loved it there. It's amazing how fast your life can change!

It was Ruthie who was responsible for my meeting Kenny. Both she and I had left our husbands after years of marriage. Throughout my journey of separation and then divorce,

Ruthie stood by my side as a best friend, cheerleader, and therapist all rolled into one. We relied on each other.

After a while, Ruthie was ready to reenter the dating world. I was not. I didn't feel the need for a man in my life. I hadn't sworn off men forever, but caring for two active girls and running a busy business left little time for anything else.

Ruthie did meet someone that she liked a lot—Bob, a fishing guide—and soon they tried to set me up with someone they thought would be a good match for me.

"I know a great guy for you!" Ruthie would tell me.

My response was always the same. "I'm not interested."

Ruthie would pester me every chance she got. "You've got to meet this guy," she coaxed me. "It's not a big deal. It'll be good for you to have a little fun."

As much as Ruthie pushed, the idea did not appeal to me. I was still grieving my marriage. Besides, I had never been on a blind date before.

"No," I told her. "I'm tired all the time and I have zero interest in listening to one more domineering male tell me how great he is."

Ruthie wouldn't give up. Finally, exasperated by my protests, she said, "Cathy, you don't have to have a relationship with the guy. You don't even have to sleep with him. It's dinner! Just dinner!"

This made me laugh and I caved. "Okay," I told her, ready to negotiate. "I will go out with this guy *one time*. But if I do, you must *never, ever* fix me up again."

"If you go," Ruthie promised, "then I will back off."

"Fine," I agreed. "But I want that in writing." Ruthie signed on the dotted line with a big dramatic flourish.

The dinner, a double date, was scheduled one week before Christmas and the evening was not at all what I expected. I liked Ruthie's beau, Bob, and I felt comfortable and at ease with the two of them—and, surprisingly, with their friend, Kenny. He was handsome, fit, a little cocky, a little flirty, and had a dazzling smile, but it was his infectious laughter and vibrant energy that intrigued me.

After dinner, I excused myself to visit the restroom. To get there, you had to follow a skinny path dotted with ferns. The path passed through a courtyard with a pretty pool. As I was walking back to the table, I bumped into Kenny along the path, and he instantly embraced me. Maybe I needed somebody to hug me, to show me some affection after so long, because I melted at once. And then he kissed me. Wow!

What the hell is happening? I thought. It was the weirdest thing—I can't explain the energy in that hug and kiss. People talk about the "spark" and "fireworks." I'd never felt that, but here it was, on a first date—a date that I hadn't even wanted to go on. This wasn't just a spark. This was an explosion, and we both felt it.

When we finally returned to the table, Bob and Ruthie were sitting there with all-knowing smirks. Kenny and I were inseparable from that point on.

I believe there are angels, and certain people are put in your life for a reason. Kenny was an angel for me. I was confused and sad when I first met him. It was becoming more and more clear to me that Larry and I had lived our whole life following a rigid plan, waiting for a reward that seemed to be unattainable and never happened. That plan was built around his wishes and only confined me. I realize now that it was also designed to keep me restricted. I was locked in a box with no friends and under the rule of a controlling and negative husband. Now, after twenty-plus years of all plan and no life, everything was different. Suddenly, I was in the company of someone who had an amazing attitude of "Let's just do it—why not?" I couldn't get enough of that positive energy.

Kenny introduced me to a whole lot of new friends and a whole lot of activities. We dined. We danced. We hiked. There were parties. There were road trips. In fact, I kept my car packed with camping gear and a variety of outfits—a dinner dress and clothes for golfing, exercise, and boating. I never knew what we'd choose to do, and when we did, I was ready. And while I was also busy with my children and my business, I didn't feel tired. I was full of energy. I was happy, happy, happy! Every day brought something new and wonderful.

As our lives were weaving together as one, making

everything and anything seem possible, there was one thing that was not possible, and Kenny had been straight with me about it from the beginning. We could not get married. Kenny had been estranged from his wife for years, but she had ALS, commonly known as Lou Gehrig's disease. And while they did not have a real marriage, and their children were grown, he also didn't feel it was right to divorce. "I can't give you a full commitment," he told me. "I don't want one," I said. After my long and miserable marriage, I wasn't looking for that.

My mother and Albert were supportive of my new relationship—although I think they worried that I was having far too much fun. I waited to introduce Kenny to my girls. They weren't seeing their father much; I actually wanted them to, but Larry didn't make the effort. So it was important for me to bring Kenny into their lives only when I was absolutely sure that our relationship was permanent. When I finally did introduce them, they loved him. You couldn't help but love Kenny.

Eventually, Kenny joined us, living at the bed-and-breakfast, and he fit right in with our family. Not only did he help me with things like driving the girls to school and back, he teased and joked, which they thought was pretty funny. Kenny could act like a big kid. If the girls didn't want to get up in the morning, he'd jump on their beds until they scrambled out, laughing. When he dropped Carmen off at school, he would honk and wave. "See you later," he'd call out, embarrassing her. He was silly, a behavior that hadn't been in our home before. He cared about the girls' interests and concerns. He cared about who they were.

The girls loved our time on *Dream Maker*, too. We took it out for sunset dinner cruises and whale-watching. They invited their friends for sleepovers and we would anchor in secluded inlets in the Vancouver Island area. We even had fun cleaning the boat, keeping it polished and shipshape.

More and more, *Dream Maker* became my refuge and affirmation that I could have a new life. At home, at the Abbotsford Classic Bed & Breakfast, I had to be the conservative mom and businesswoman. But on the water, I truly relaxed. An easy drive brought me to the marina, where *Dream Maker* was waiting for me, where my friends joined me, and where Kenny treated me with affection, encouragement, and love.

It was incredible to me that I now had so many new friends. Kenny was on two baseball teams and he played twice a week, so all of a sudden I was part of a big group. Like Kenny, they welcomed me with open arms. I felt I belonged somewhere.

Kenny lived with no regrets and believed that you only live life once, so you might as well live it! There was no doing anything halfway with Kenny. "Cathy, if you're not living on the edge," he told me one day, "you're just wasting space." I was finally beginning to understand what this really meant. I was allowing Kenny's ideas, his enthusiasm, and his huge heart to change mine. I was not only changing, I was thriving.

The truth is, your life might end tomorrow, so why not make *today* better? Why not live today the best you can? Why not make a memory? And that's what we did. In fact, we made memories for other people too.

One weekend we were headed to Salt Spring Island. We'd heard about a posh restaurant on the island, so we made a reservation and decided we'd stay overnight and go home the next day. When we arrived, Kenny asked the guy working the marina dock, "Can we leave our boat docked here or do we have to move?" And the guy told him, "You can't dock here, you have to move."

Now, I've got to stop here a minute to tell you that for this special excursion, Kenny had bought me a new outfit to wear to dinner, which included an attractive Tommy Bahama shirt. He knew we'd need to be appropriately dressed for the four-course meal in the elegant dining room. He'd also bought me new earrings, and I'd gone ahead and fixed up my hair with extra care and had my nails painted. Our reservation wasn't for another hour, so when we were told we couldn't dock, we figured it was no big deal. We'd have plenty of time to moor the boat offshore and then take our dinghy back to the restaurant.

Kenny was preparing to back *Dream Maker* out of the marina, and I was on the pier untying the line at the bow from the piling. Just in that moment, Kenny (due to his lack of boating experience) gunned the engine in reverse and I (a novice with unsteady sea legs) fell off the dock as the line jerked in my hand.

So there I was in the ocean, floundering in my nice new shirt. I'm short, five-foot-two, and I couldn't reach high enough to grab the ladder on the pier. I don't know where they came from, but lucky for me, two guys grabbed my wrists and hauled me out of the water like the catch of the day.

Everybody watching thought it was a pretty funny sight. I couldn't get angry with Kenny. I was more worried about ruining the new shirt that he'd bought me and about showing up to a fancy dinner with wet hair.

I was the talk of the island—the "drowned rat" who fell off the dock while untying *Dream Maker*—and my celebrity spread, because the next day when I went to take my clothes to the dry cleaner, the man at the counter said, "Oh, you're *that* lady."

After that, we reviewed our new cardinal rule—usually while laughing: *Don't hit the gas when you're going in reverse!* I think there's a lesson to be learned from that for lots of situations in life, don't you?

Kenny and I were solid. We couldn't imagine a life without each other. So I took another big step and decided to put my house and business in Abbotsford up for sale. We planned to move to White Rock to be closer to the marina and *Dream Maker*. The girls approved of the idea, and Kenny and I both had jobs waiting with his employer. In the meantime, we spent our free time hopping from island to island, meeting all kinds of people.

I remember on one such outing we were lost. (No surprise there—in our explorations, getting lost often happened.) But it wasn't a big deal. There was no stress about it; it was all part of the adventure. Kenny's attitude when such things happened was "How bad can it be?" and "We'll figure it out."

This time, we found ourselves just off an island on the Sunshine Coast. We came upon another boat, which was anchored. Kenny yelled out to them, "Excuse me, can you tell us where we are?" The guy on the other boat thought this was quite hilarious. And after a few friendly exchanges, Kenny asked, "What are you doing?"

"We just got married," the guy answered. "We came here all the way from Salt Lake City."

We could see on the hillside what looked like a golf course, so Kenny yelled, "Is there a golf course here?"

"You bet," said the guy. "Do you golf?"

Kenny said, "You bet!"

The next thing you know, despite my worries about intruding on the couple's honeymoon, we'd anchored alongside their boat and made instant friends. One hour later, we were golfing as a foursome. And after that, having a great time at dinner. The husband was very much like Kenny. He'd rented this yacht for their honeymoon, but he'd never even had a boating course. The rental company would not let him take the boat out unless he could dock the boat three times in a row. They taught him. He did it, and now he was out on this boat having a blast with his new wife . . . and us.

I've come to learn that boaters, both the experienced and the novices, tend to be friendly. There is a sense of camaraderie when you meet on the water; nothing is formal, and people are approachable and welcoming.

I think the best time on *Dream Maker*, the most cherished memory for me, was when we were in the Juan de Fuca Strait. We were cruising slowly in the moonlight. The water was phosphorescent. I was mesmerized by the bow wave as it gradually turned into a glowing wake spreading out behind us. Beyond the wake were the beautiful islands that dot this scenic waterway. I will never forget that phosphorescence in the moonlight. I thought, *Now, if this isn't making a memory, what is?*

Little did I know it would be one of the last with Kenny.

In the spirit of making a memory and living life to the fullest, I went for the boat I dreamed of (which happened to be called *Dream Maker*), admittedly after some nudging from Kenny. I never once regretted that decision. It was the best present I could have ever given to my daughters and to myself. Our boat opened up a whole new world, and offered so much fun and freedom for all of us.

My previous carefully laid plans had gotten me to where

I was, and I do believe that it is important to stick with a goal, but there is also a time and place for indulging in spontaneity. Until I met Kenny, that was something I never felt able to act on. That life lesson was invaluable and just what I needed.

Your dream doesn't have to be a boat. The memories you make may never be on the ocean. Your dream doesn't have to be big and luxurious. You might hope to take your kids camping, or take a pottery or singing class, or learn to cook Chinese food. Every woman and man has something they've always wanted to do—a dream that they emotionally connect to. It's easy to dismiss that impulse, to rationalize that you shouldn't because you can't afford it, or the timing isn't right, or it's just plain silly. I've come to believe that if your dream is something that will give you happiness, you must find a way to make it happen. **Make a memory.**

EXERCISES

When you find yourself running blindly from what you are afraid of, stop and ask yourself: *Can I overcome this problem? If I can't do it by myself, can I find someone to help?*

List at least three specific times in your life when you've run blindly from something you were afraid of:

1. _____
   _____
   _____
   _____

2. _____
   _____
   _____
   _____

3. _____
   _____
   _____
   _____

Now, briefly describe what you did or who you called to help you do whatever it took to overcome the fear. (This is a MOST important step for you to see your dreams come true.)

CHAPTER 8

TOTALLY LOST

We drove along the Sea-to-Sky Highway, which runs from Vancouver to Whistler, with scenic ocean views and soaring mountains along the way, headed to one of Kenny's baseball games. Kenny was as excited as a little boy. The game was being held in the charming town of Squamish at the north end of Howe Sound, a little less than two hours from Abbotsford.

This small community, with Mount Garibaldi rising in the background, is heavily populated by Native Americans/ First Nations peoples. It's no surprise, then, that the beautifully carved totem poles of their native cultures are everywhere. When we passed the first totem pole, with eagle wings spread wide, it reminded me of how I would tease Kenny, whose tanned complexion, high cheekbones, and handsome square jaw suggested that he might be descended from Native ancestry. "You're home," I said to him as I reached to place my hand on his.

When we arrived, the game was about to begin. Kenny joined his teammates on the field, and I joined the other buddies, wives, and families in the stands, ready to cheer the team on. I could tell that, as usual, Kenny was all fired up and eager to play. It was a beautiful day and we were all glad to be there.

Normally, Kenny played shortstop, but today the coach changed his position to second base. Kenny looked up in the stands to see whether I had noticed the change. To communicate back that indeed I had, I thought I'd send him a special, spontaneous message. Since I was wearing my bikini top under my shirt, and since no one seemed to be paying much attention . . . I flashed him. It was like a thumbs-up. *Your biggest fan is right here watching!* Kenny loved it.

The first player stepped up to bat and the woman standing next to me began to cheer. I turned to her to offer some friendly remarks, when I was interrupted by screaming and yelling from the field. This didn't sound like baseball cheers, and I looked back to the diamond to see what all the ruckus was about. What I saw was someone lying on the ground. I jumped from my seat and ran from the stands to the field as fast as I could.

When I got closer, I saw that it was my Kenny lying there. I lost it. Now the screaming was coming out of my mouth. Strangers tried to calm me down, to hold me back, but I refused. Nothing would keep me from him. It was all so unreal. *What was happening?!*

My mind was spinning, trying to make sense of this horrible moment. A jumble of thoughts rushed in. Wasn't it just two weeks ago that a bruise had appeared over Kenny's heart where a baseball had slammed into him? "I'm getting too old for this," he joked to me. "I'd better stop playing or this game is going to kill me." Of course, he hadn't meant a word of it. He had no intention of not playing.

And just this morning at breakfast, hadn't he complained of heartburn? I'd kidded him about the lively party we'd been to the night before. "You're probably still recovering from those shots of tequila," I said. Kenny had laughed. I offered him a Tums and we left for the game.

Hadn't he also complained that his arm was bothering him? But he didn't seem to mind and we didn't make any connection.

Now he was on the ground. It must have been a heart attack. I know CPR, but instead of leaping into action, I froze. *What if I do it wrong? What if I mess up somehow and hurt him more?*

I kept thinking of Grace, one of my bed-and-breakfast guests and one of the loveliest ladies I've ever met. She had shared with me a story about her adult son, who had suffered a heart attack and then brain damage when his heart couldn't be resuscitated fast enough. "He was never the same," Grace told me. Now her words repeated in my head. *He was never the same.*

This cannot happen to Kenny. Kenny can't become a vegetable. Not him! Not this man with his tremendous passion for life. Not Kenny! All these colliding thoughts immobilized me with fear and I was afraid to touch him.

"Does anyone know CPR?" I shouted in panic, but my cries were unnecessary, as strangers I didn't know had come forward and were already trying to revive him.

The ambulance seemed to take hours to come.

"This is taking too long," I kept shouting. "It's taking too long." *God, if he goes too long, just take him.* I knew Kenny would rather die than sit in a room paralyzed, unable to speak or move.

When the paramedics did arrive in the ambulance, they whisked Kenny off to the local ER. The next thing I clearly remember was sitting next to him as he lay in a hospital bed. The lights were low and I held his hand. I understood instinctively that this Kenny was not the man I had known for the last two and a half years.

"I'm afraid he's not going to make it," the doctor said to me. "We've tried everything. There is nothing else medically I can do." And then he added the most dreaded words. "Should we disconnect him from life support?"

This doctor was asking me whether to pull the plug. Kenny was going to die. I thought, *You cannot ask me to do that. I cannot do that.* "I can't make that decision," I finally stammered. "You need to do that. You're the doctor. You're in charge."

"You have to make this call," the doctor answered softly.

But I could not do this. Neither emotionally nor legally. Kenny's family was called and made the necessary decisions and arrangements. I remained in that darkened hospital room with the man I profoundly loved. Kenny had given me a life. Now, he had been pronounced dead. I could not comprehend that fact.

I was totally lost. Devastated. There were no words.

Perhaps you have experienced overwhelming loss, found yourself in a place of deep and unrelenting sadness. Perhaps, as I did, you felt there would be no recovering from the darkness. Even if we tirelessly search for an explanation, a reason to help us make sense of the unfathomable, we don't always find it. For me, I only began to find comfort and healing in something I'd always known—the knowledge that Kenny was a great blessing in my life. A gift. For that, I am forever grateful.

EXERCISES

When you have a significant problem or issue to overcome, who is an objective friend or professional who can help you evaluate your situation and make appropriate changes? Everyone needs help and assistance at some point in their life. An emotional pain or a critical decision that needs to be made is often more difficult than a physical pain or disease. List at least three professional or objective persons whom you choose to turn to for assistance.

1. _____
2. _____
3. _____

CHAPTER 9

WHEN THINGS FALL APART

Kenny was dead. Suddenly, shockingly dead, and my new and joyous life was turned upside down in a flash.

Kenny's time was cut short and it seemed so unfair. Every ounce of my being was filled with an unspeakable grief, and yet, I had no idea how much pain was still to come over the next year. Many times the sorrow was more than I thought I could bear. I also knew that I must take care of my girls. They were devastated too. I had to be strong for them. I had to lead the way.

My daughter Caitlin slept with me, to comfort me, because nights were the most difficult—all I did was cry. (I will forever be grateful to her for this.) Carmen was crushed. When I first introduced Kenny to my girls, Carmen made life difficult for him. "You're not my dad," she'd remind him in the sassy tone that fourteen-year-olds are infamous for, and she'd stomp off mid-sentence when he spoke or asked a question. Kenny took it all in stride and eventually won her over; he ended up being her great ally. In fact, the very weekend that Kenny died, Carmen was away on a camping trip. It was a trip that included a boy whom Carmen had a crush on. When Carmen first proposed the trip, my response was "Absolutely not!" Kenny had come to her aid, though, and persuaded me to let Carmen go. Now she had returned home to find him gone forever. The loss of Kenny left a huge hole in all our hearts.

When I left the hospital where Kenny died, I returned to Abbotsford and never felt so alone. My best friend was missing. Kenny's brother, whom I had met only once before, arrived and stayed at my bed-and-breakfast while he made arrangements with Kenny's family for the funeral.

I didn't feel up to all the tough decisions, but I got involved because I wanted, most of all, for Kenny's life to be properly remembered and celebrated. We weren't married legally, but I felt we were married in our hearts. I knew that he had felt the same.

My dealings with Kenny's brother felt strange and, unfortunately, became uncomfortable and tense. I was still trying to digest Kenny's death while his family was hoping to claim bits of him. His son wanted his car. His brother wanted his clothes. They wanted everything that was his. Relatives I didn't know came and went in and out of my home at all hours. I just wanted Kenny back.

In those brief times when the house was empty, I cried.

It seemed like that was all I was good for. Crying. And more crying.

Two days before the funeral, things came to a head with Kenny's brother. We argued about Kenny's burial clothes. The brother wanted him to be buried in a suit. I was determined that Kenny would not be wearing any kind of a suit. He wasn't a suit person. He would have hated that! Kenny's brother and I went back and forth, round and round, but I absolutely would not back down. *They can plan the funeral. They can take his things. They can do whatever else they want, but Kenny* will not *be wearing a suit.*

In the end, Kenny was dressed in a pair of green pants that I had bought him and his favorite shirt—the Tommy Bahama shirt, the one that matched mine.

Even though I didn't want to, I gave Kenny's brother all of Kenny's clothes as a gesture to smooth things over. It broke my heart. When you've lost a loved one, their familiar smell stays on their clothes, and you want to hang on to the garments. It's an attempt to hang on to the loved one.

When my daughters and I entered the funeral home, it felt like a time warp. All the pictures displayed portrayed Kenny and his family ten years earlier. It was as if the life he had with us had never existed. Caitlin saw Kenny's wife's friend walk up to the flower arrangement my family had sent and remove our sympathy card. They were trying to erase all memory of our existence.

Seeing Kenny in a coffin brought back every bit of the pain that I felt when he was pronounced dead—even more so. It seared me. I brought a photo with me to the funeral home. The photo showed the two of us wearing our matching shirts. My last expression of love to Kenny was to slip this photo under his shirt and place it on his chest above his heart. Kenny will always have a place in *my* heart and I wanted to keep a physical reminder of our life together near to his.

By the end of the service, I was in a fog. I refused to go downstairs to the reception with his family because of the way they had treated us. I was last to leave the funeral home. Two close friends, Bob and Mark, came back inside and escorted me out. To my surprise, there were over 300 people waiting to greet me in the parking lot. I was so grateful for that show of support.

Afterward, I held a wake for Kenny at his favorite restaurant. All of Kenny's friends were there. There was food, laughter, and memories. I think Kenny would have liked that. But to my dismay, his estranged wife showed up. I was utterly shocked.

Kenny was cremated. His family had not wanted to share the ashes, but the funeral guy was kind enough to give me some anyway. I placed them in a beautiful, eagle-shaped urn. This is where his ashes still remain.

In the beginning, each day after I dropped the girls off at school, I went to White Rock and walked the promenade and cried. *Why did you leave me? Why? Why?* Of course, there was no answer that could satisfy me. I've since learned that sometimes the hardest questions don't get answers.

I couldn't bring myself to go to *Dream Maker*. The boat had really been our house and it was too much for me to step on board. But walking the promenade, back and forth next to the water, gave me a small sense of comfort.

When a loved one dies, things fall apart. It's a complete collapse. Time stops. Life as you know it stops. It seems impossible to make sense of anything. Even if there were something or someone to blame (and there wasn't), no one could bring back Kenny. And that is all I wanted. Kenny.

I did have many wonderful memories, and they were a gift, but I knew nothing would ever be the same. There would be no going backward. I could only try to move forward, small step by small step. I found moments of comfort where I could—from my close friends, my family, and nature's healing waters—from the predictable, rhythmic Semiahmoo Bay waves that, in time, began to soothe my aching heart.

Dream Maker

Carmen wrote this poem for Kenny
and read it at his wake.

Have you ever sailed along the sandy beach,
With the cold crisp waters grasping tight on your feet?
Or with the warm brisk wind blowing in your hair,
With waves so high and mighty it would give you a scare?

The fish would be jumping about five feet high,
When you're resting on the bow looking up in the sunny sky.
The captain of the boat would be drifting five knots an hour,
When he boosts it up a couple speeds to get more power.

You're sailing along with the love of your life,
Relaxing in heat, and boiling in sunlight.
You sway to the shore where everything is set,
And you turn to the captain that was bathing in sweat.

You set up camp for the rest of the night,
Then you sit down by the fire, and look around at the site.
It starts to chill, the sun is gone for now,
Where you and your soul mate snuggle tight and make a vow.

The dark night comes slashing through day,
Where your soul mate or companion turns to you and says . . .

You are the love of my life, that will always be;
I will miss you forever, just wait and see.
I can't get through life without thinking of you.
If you die, we will meet again in heaven, sometime soon.

I would try not to grieve every second of the day;
I would be here for now, that's where I'll stay.
But nothing lasts forever, I have learned.
I would make it through life;
There's no need to be concerned.

I just want you to remember, with all of your heart,
That I will always love you,
And we will never part.

EXERCISES

Not "if," but "when," someone or something significant in your life dies, how can you trust that hope and good things will eventually prove that emptiness and loss is only temporary? This is a hard question and one to answer from your heart rather than from your head.

CHAPTER 10

THE POWER OF INSTINCT

In the months following Kenny's funeral, I was depressed. More than depressed. Laughter, fun, and hopes for a positive future had vanished. Those days are a blur to me now, but I remember how difficult it was to accomplish even the smallest task. I was trying hard to care for my daughters and my business. It seemed there was so much work to do, the bed-and-breakfast guests to tend to, and errands to run. Even getting out of bed was difficult. Just thinking about all that had to be done wore me out. I was emotionally and physically exhausted.

I was also still baffled by life. It seemed that one moment all was rolling along nicely. You're feeling on top of the world, confident that you've accomplished some important goals, and the future looks bright. In the next moment, your hopes and dreams are gone. Nothing left except the shattered pieces of what used to be.

Here's what I've learned: Everything can crumble, and when it does, you may get knocked down hard. Most of us do at some point, and it's the getting up that makes all the difference. When you're down, really down, it's hard to know which way to turn, what to do, and whom you can trust. I trusted Kenny. We'd been together almost three years. I trusted the life lessons he taught me. Kenny taught me to take chances and think outside the box. He taught me that it's okay to want to have a full life, that it's okay to have fun. He taught me that I didn't always have to have a detailed plan. This was the strength I needed and so I decided to trust and honor his lessons. I decided to run with this advice.

I sold *Dream Maker*. I pretty much just gave the boat away. I couldn't emotionally manage it on my own, but I did carry on with the plan Kenny and I had made to move to White Rock. I sold my bed-and-breakfast and went. The girls were eleven and fifteen. They were still young enough that I could get them started in school so that they could make good friends, and they were agreeable to the idea. I began getting freelance marketing jobs in Vancouver. I also leased four houses with ocean views in the White Rock area and rented them out weekly and monthly. I turned one of the leased buildings into a gift shop.

I wanted to buy and not lease my own home. As a self-employed, divorced single mom, I was viewed as a risk,

I guess, by the banks: Thirteen of them turned down my loan application. I was no longer the kind of woman who took no for an answer. The fourteenth bank approved the loan. Still, I was short $10,000 for the house I had set my sights on.

It is quite amazing that just after your darkest hours, when you begin to peek out into the world, you'll find support all around you. My wonderful bed-and-breakfast guest, Grace, was staying with me when Kenny died. She really understood what I was going through, since she had a son who had suffered a heart attack and resulting brain damage and who was now in a home. Grace loaned me the $10,000 that I needed and I bought my home in White Rock.

While White Rock is not far from Abbotsford, I felt like it was a world away. None of this happened overnight, but I kept at it and made the changes I thought were necessary for the girls and me to begin once again.

There was another unexpected person who popped into my life and helped me heal—Kenny's friend Chuck. Kenny had lots of friends and Chuck was not a longtime buddy, but when they met, they connected right away. In fact, I was with Kenny when he first met Chuck.

Kenny and I were at a boating friend's afternoon barbeque, and there was an American guy from Las Vegas there who kept a condo in Vancouver. He was a good-looking man, about five-foot-seven, with sandy hair, blue eyes, and a pearly white smile. Kenny was never shy in any situation, and he always welcomed anyone new into our group of friends, and so he walked right up to Chuck and introduced himself. They hit it off immediately and became good pals right away, which looking back on it now doesn't surprise me at all.

Kenny was an extrovert; he could be loud and noisy. Chuck is not as eccentric and is rather quiet, even shy, but both men are spontaneous. They both believe in living life to the fullest. It seemed like there wasn't anything that this guy Chuck didn't do—boating, riding motorcycles, flying helicopters. Kenny thought all of this was fantastic, but I was skeptical at first. I'd never met anybody who could do so many different things. Plus, he told Kenny that he ran a business that provided services to locate buried utility lines. I thought, *How is all of this possible? It can't be right.*

Kenny somehow also learned that first day they met— how this came up, I have no idea—that my birthday (September 23) is one day before Chuck's. It was just like Kenny to seize the moment. "Good news, Cathy," he announced after he returned from talking with Chuck. "We're going to Vegas for your birthday."

"What?" I said. "You've got to be kidding me."

Kenny fired right back, anticipating my concerns. "It's going to be great, really great! You'll see. We're going to stay at Chuck's house in Vegas because your birthdays are only one day apart."

"Stay at Chuck's house? You've just met this guy," I protested.

But Kenny, in his usual fashion, wasn't fazed and was

always up for a new adventure. "Don't worry," he assured me. "It'll be fine. We'll all have a great time. If you don't like it, I promise that we'll leave."

I didn't think a sincere invitation to someone's house could happen that quickly, but Kenny coaxed me to meet his new friend. And so as the sun began to set over the barbeque and the drinks kept flowing, I didn't want to spoil the fun and I humored them both. "Sure, let's go to Vegas!"

We did go! I was nervous. I'd never been to Las Vegas and I heard the crime was terrible and I still wasn't sure about this Chuck. Who was he anyway? What kind of person lives in Vegas? Frankly, I was still suspicious that this active, self-made man was too good to be true. What was the catch?

Chuck's neighborhood was in a gated community. These were not small houses. A guard greeted us, and as I looked around, I was reminded of glossy magazine pictures and the grand houses in movies. Each house was like the Ritz-Carlton.

We drove farther down the street and saw Chuck's home. There was only one word for it. *Huge.* Kenny and I walked into the entrance hallway and I thought, *Oh, my, the entryway of this house is bigger than my kitchen.* Of course, I tried to play it cool, like this was the kind of place I went every day, but I'm sure the look on my face, my big eyes, and my open mouth gave me away. I was seriously impressed.

The trip to Vegas cemented the friendship between Kenny and Chuck. Yes, we were wined and dined and had an excellent birthday celebration. Still, I wasn't completely sold and remained skeptical. The two men shared a spontaneous, adventurous spirit, and over the next year, it seemed to me that every time they met up, Kenny lost his common sense. Kenny was more than smart, but his practicality almost vanished when Chuck came around. You never knew what the two of them were going to cook up.

Kenny worked hard and made a good living, but he also loved to splurge. He liked to live like a millionaire. "Cathy, it'll be fun to be millionaires for the day," he'd say. Even though he was low-key about it and not showy or pretentious, Chuck really was a millionaire, so he had no problem with agreeing to spur-of-the-moment trips, boating excursions, or helicopter rides. It all appealed to Kenny, but unlike his new friend, these were not always things that Kenny could afford. But he would still strive to live life like a millionaire—even if it was only for a day—just to have that memory.

I held Kenny's hand in the hospital the day that he died and I kept asking for Chuck. The doctor kept pushing me to make the decision, but I couldn't answer.

"Somebody get Chuck! Please find Chuck! I need him! Please find Chuck!" I'm told I repeated these requests over and over. There were many people who could have helped me, and Chuck wouldn't have been an obvious choice for me. But instinctively, I kept asking for Kenny's friend.

Chuck had gone to the party with us the night before Kenny died, and Chuck had driven to Squamish for the game, but he hadn't arrived in time for the game and was not there to see Kenny collapse. I do not know who went and found Chuck, but he appeared at the hospital and stayed by my side. He was the one who drove me home on that incredibly sad day. Chuck and I said very little. It was the hardest, most difficult trip of my life. I'd left Kenny at the hospital. I was going home without him.

I think we've all got a sixth sense, a human instinct that can't be explained. At least I can't explain it. But those feelings are there and are hard to deny. You might feel it when you meet someone for the first time and yet it feels like you've known this person for years. Or, you could find yourself momentarily in jeopardy, but you somehow sense that everything will be okay. You're not absolutely sure of the outcome, but your instinct is powerful and reassuring. On some level, that is how Chuck made me feel when he came to the hospital.

I've learned to pay attention to patterns and signs in my life. Looking back through the years, so many people and places, I realize now, fit together like puzzle pieces. Many of my relationships and major life events are somehow linked, though I did not know it at the time, and could never have dreamed how things in my life would turn out.

In the months prior to his death, Kenny had made some odd comments to me. "I think you and Chuck would be good together," he would tease me. I would tell him to cut it out.

It's possible that Kenny's comments about Chuck were only coincidence. But I don't believe that. I believe that God somehow used Kenny to place these thoughts in my head, long before I was ready to hear them.

I know that Kenny and I loved each other deeply, but did Kenny sense that his life was to end soon? Did he want to know that I would be okay and happy? I'm guessing that this is probably why, as I held Kenny's lifeless hand, I knew, subconsciously, that he wanted me to reach out to Chuck for comfort and help. And although I don't remember calling for Chuck on that horrible day, it is apparently exactly what I did.

You may not know why people come into your life, or why a person who does not figure significantly now one day becomes important. Whether this involves business, or guidance, or a relationship, unexpected opportunities will appear. All I know is that for these things to occur, you have to be open enough to recognize and receive them.

EXERCISES

List at least two tangible dreams that you see happening in your life because you made a conscious choice to keep the blinders on and not look back, kept making progress and just did it, and never, never quit. Don't hold back on your dreams and the actions you take, so that your dreams can indeed come true! Why not?

1. _____
   _____
   _____
   _____
   _____
   _____
   _____
   _____

2. _____
   _____
   _____
   _____
   _____
   _____
   _____

CHAPTER 11

NEW BEGINNINGS

Sooner or later, things do change. For you, me, everyone—everything keeps moving and changing. Evolving. If you're open to positive change and new beginnings rather than waiting to "get back to normal," good things will eventually happen. Frankly, it's easier to stay stuck; however, I believe it is well worth it to dig deep inside yourself: to face your fears, pick up, and start all over again.

I felt lost and lonely for more than a year after Kenny's death. It's like being in a crowded room of people but feeling like you're the only one there. Even a simple conversation could seem impossible. I remember wondering, *Who can possibly understand what's happening to me?*

I did not hear from Chuck after the day he appeared at the hospital and took me home. He did not come to Kenny's funeral. He did not call me on our September birthdays.

It was a disappointment because I thought he might be someone who could understand. Then, out of the blue, four months later he called me up to say hi.

"I'm in town," he announced. By this time, I was living in White Rock and I couldn't imagine why, after all this time, he was phoning me now.

"What are you doing tomorrow?" he asked. "I'm selling my condo in Vancouver, packing the place up. Want to come with me?"

We spent the day in Vancouver and he took the opportunity to explain his silence. He had felt uncomfortable about calling to check on me.

That day, we didn't do anything extraordinary. There were no grand trips or adventures. I helped him pack up the last of his condo, we went to Chinatown, and we talked. It was the first time I had felt normal in months. Chuck was the only person who seemed to understand my ongoing grief. What did happen on that day in Vancouver is that we became friends. Now I felt he wasn't just Kenny's friend. He was my friend too.

Chuck made several trips to visit me. It felt nice to have someone to talk to. The first time he instinctively grabbed my hand, it felt weird. I also noticed that I had butterflies. And those feelings complicated everything for me. I couldn't help feeling I was cheating on Kenny.

Chuck never pushed me to deepen our relationship. He knew I was still grieving. What I hadn't really recognized was that he was too. "You're not the only one who misses him," he reminded me. "Remember, I've lost a best friend." The moment he said it, I knew it was true.

As Chuck and I began slowly developing a closer friendship, I felt the need to trust him, really trust him. I guess I was afraid of my new feelings, and some of the old doubts crept into my mind. The truth is, I was having romantic feelings for Chuck. It made me jittery and afraid. I had been through enough already. Another relationship loss just wasn't an option.

I knew Chuck was successful, and I knew him to be kind, but I needed the assurance that his business affairs and his personal life were all that he said they were. There were no specific reasons to make me think otherwise, but before I jumped into this, I wanted to know that his business life was legitimate and that there wasn't a string of girlfriends lurking around on the sidelines. My fears weren't based in any reality, because Chuck would always answer any question I had, was always straightforward, but I felt the need to check it out firsthand. I imagine I was trying to protect myself from any further unhappiness, disappointment, and loss. I'd had my heart broken more than once. Now I wanted to be cautious.

I did something incredibly spontaneous. The girls were scheduled to visit their father, and after I dropped them off, I decided to make a surprise trip to visit Chuck, who now lived in Salt Lake City. I had just enough money and time to make the flight. "I will only stay three days," I promised myself. This was a major ordeal, and I was nervous, but I also had to admit that I was excited and full of anticipation.

Landing in Salt Lake City, I had no idea where Chuck lived or where to find him. So I called his cell phone from the airport, and when he answered, I said two words: "I'm here."

I'm sure his jaw dropped to the floor, and he replied, "You're where?"

"I'm here," I said with a laugh, unable to contain my excitement. "I'm in Salt Lake, and I'm here to see you."

Of course, my ulterior motive for coming was truth-checking, to prove to myself that everything I knew about Chuck, that everything he told me was true, was on the up-and-up. I knew that this trip was a surprise attack, but at the same time I was so happy to see him. I hoped he would be happy to see me too.

He was. Chuck was telling the truth, and what I learned on my fact-finding adventure finally put me at ease. On the phone, Chuck gave me directions to his house, and as I drove up the drive, he stood in front of his log cabin home in the mountains. I had barely stepped out of the car when Chuck wrapped me in his arms. "You must be hungry," he said. "How about if I make you dinner?"

It felt as if I were home.

The next day we decided to go Christmas shopping. Chuck was divorced, but all of his children and grandchildren were visiting later in the month for the holidays. Gifts needed to be bought. I helped Chuck buy a ton of presents, mostly toys, and I loved every minute of it. It felt like this was something that we should be doing together, like we were family.

Our relationship continued to grow. We visited back and forth from Salt Lake City to White Rock. My friend Ruthie was also in love. She was marrying her boyfriend, Bob. She wanted me to stand up for her. When I mentioned to Chuck that I was going to Mexico for the wedding, he wanted to go too. He liked Ruthie and was happy for her. Who would have thought that Chuck would be standing up for her new husband instead of Kenny?

The trip was great, but it also reminded me of a deeper sadness that I still carried. It was impossible not to think of Kenny and I couldn't shake the guilt I felt about dating Chuck. I didn't want to break it off, but I was unsettled and confused.

Chuck asked me to join him for a horse-riding trip to Jackson Hole, Wyoming. I had been riding before, but that was quite a long time ago, and I hadn't done it much. Of course, I would never admit to my inexperience, so I said, "Yeah, I can ride a horse. No problem."

Before long, I was riding on the back of a horse and inching up a scenic mountain trail, with a packhorse close behind. We climbed higher and higher, winding our way up the mountain. The vistas from the trail were spectacular. Still, there was one detail I hadn't counted on, which I discovered only hours into our four-day riding trip: When you're riding a horse as a beginner—and riding, riding, and then riding more—you can begin to feel sore in the saddle. I was enjoying myself, but, wow! That takes some getting used to.

At the end of the first day, we had ridden many miles and stopped to make our camp for the night. It was the greatest feeling. Horseback riding, a campfire, sleeping outside underneath a clear, star-filled sky—it doesn't get much better than that. I felt close to and protected by nature—the covering trees, the open sky, the solid ground—and I felt so close to Chuck. I really had strong feelings for this man. I thought, *Oh, my God. This guy is so cool, so accomplished*, and I realized lying below that umbrella of shining stars that I was actually feeling happy again. Something within me was beginning to shift.

On the fourth day, we traveled back down the mountain trail. At the bottom, we said our good-byes to the horses and then stopped to eat at, of all places, the Cowboy Bar. We walked in and it was packed, wall-to-wall people. No tables or chairs were left and we had to sit at the bar. On saddles! *You've got to be joking*, I thought. *I've been riding on a horse for four days. I'm tired and sore. How the hell am I going to sit on a barstool that's a saddle?* I decided to sit aside rather than astride in this saddle, with both of my legs draped over one side.

"English sidesaddle," I said to Chuck. We both had a good laugh.

Chuck isn't extroverted, but he is, in his way, always open to everyone. He's generous, too. With Chuck, it's give, give, give. Almost to a fault. I wasn't used to that and it was something else that made me nervous at first. I learned that I had to be careful about what I asked for.

For instance, on one of his visits to White Rock, Chuck,

who loves motorcycles, was telling me about the Sturgis Motorcycle Rally in South Dakota every August. To get there, riders travel through places like Black Hills National Forest (past Mt. Rushmore and Crazy Horse Memorial) and the Badlands. At the rally, there are races, bike shows, and concerts. I had never been on a motorcycle and I said, "Wow, how wonderful that would be! Wouldn't it be cool if we got a Harley and rode to Sturgis?"

I hadn't been serious. There are lots of things that sound like fun to me but I don't expect to do them. In what seemed like two seconds, Chuck and I were in a Harley dealership buying a bike. Then he said, "Cathy, the Harley is yours." That's right. Mine!

I said, "What? The Harley is whose?" With a boyish grin, Chuck said, "It's yours. I want you to have your own bike. You said you wanted to learn to ride."

"I guess I said that . . . "

So, Chuck bought me a Harley-Davidson Heritage Softail Classic motorcycle and I accepted the gift and the challenge to learn to ride. After that, I was more careful about what I said I wanted.

I was now the owner of this huge bike. It was sitting in my garage and I had no clue how to ride it. What to do? By the end of the month, I had signed up for motorcycle lessons, taken both the written and the driving test, and passed. That's it. I had a motorcycle and a license, and we were about to drive to Sturgis, South Dakota. Who would have thought?

In preparation, Chuck and I made two short drives in my area with fellow motorcycle lovers. Riding with others in the community in a large group was invigorating. The energy from those group rides was incredible. It was so cool to be part of something big.

I was now thinking about the long ride from Canada to Sturgis. All we could talk about was "the trip, the trip, the trip." Chuck bought me all the leathers, the riding coat, and the gear. I was psyched for this trip. I was feeling like my old self: adventurous again. I wasn't aware of the moment it happened—I guess it was a gradual process—but I was ready to be out in the world.

My girls were all set, staying with their regular and favorite babysitter. They liked Chuck and were excited for me. For sure, he was different from the exuberant Kenny and they noticed that right away. Chuck can be so quiet. You can't but compare. Chuck spent time with the girls and took them places so that they could have new experiences again, such as skiing. Like me, they came to love him.

So now, my boyfriend and I were riding to one of the largest bike rallies in the world. It seemed unreal. Could such things really be happening to me?

When you begin to fall in love again after losing someone, you feel guilty. After many years, I understand that it's not wrong to love more than one person in your life. In the beginning, it was a struggle for me. Chuck understood this and never held it against me.

After Kenny died, I had no interest in getting involved with anyone romantically. Guys asked me out, but I didn't want to go. I had no intention of dating Chuck either, but he was one of the few people who could truly understand why I was so sad. Chuck has never acted jealous about Kenny. He never said, "Don't talk about all that." In fact, he will bring up Kenny more than I do.

I didn't have to hide any of my feelings. Chuck made sure that Kenny was included in our lives. "I wish Kenny could see this," he'd say to me. "Kenny would love this."

As I said before, if you are open, there will be unexpected opportunities that pop up in your life. There will be places where you can find support, and guidance, and even love again.

One night in Chuck's mountain cabin in Utah, all the power went out in the area. It was total blackness. All of a sudden, the fluorescent lights in the cabin's ceiling flickered on and off a few times and then stayed on for the night while every other light remained dark. It made no sense that these lights were on, that they stayed on. There was no reason for it.

"That's Kenny checking on us," I joked to Chuck. "You'd better be nice."

"I will," Chuck said.

Although I had said this as a joke, we both felt that Kenny was somehow with us that night, communicating that all was okay, that he would be watching out for us.

CHAPTER 12

DON'T GO IT ALONE

I'd come to enjoy riding motorcycles. I loved the outdoors. I loved the sense of freedom. Most of all, I loved being with Chuck. This time, we were riding together on my beautiful Harley. I was seated behind Chuck, watching the sun reflect off the bike's shiny chrome.

We were on our way to another Harley rally in Wisconsin, and at the moment, we were passing through southeastern Montana. While Montana is near the Canadian border, I was amazed that this section of the state had the kind of landscape you'd expect to find in Arizona—arid rolling country, desert and shrubland.

Along the way we'd met Steve and George, two guys who were also on Harleys, and we joined them at a small Cheyenne Indian Reservation bar. The biker community is similar to boaters; you meet up unexpectedly, making friends fast. Once inside the bar, our leather gear made it obvious that we were strangers there. After a dinner break, a handful of locals who were also hanging out in the bar returned with us to the parking lot. They were fascinated by the Harleys and wanted to touch and sit on each of the bikes. We obliged.

Steve, who looked like he belonged on a Harley (tall, bald, broad shoulders, and lots of tattoos), did most of the talking, and was now hurrying it along so the four of us could be on our way.

An old shaman came up to us and approached Steve first. "You have a safe ride. The road out there is . . ." The shaman stopped short. "Wait," he said, as if something important had just occurred to him. He then turned and walked up to Chuck. "You have a safe ride, Captain," he said, looking Chuck directly in the eye.

When the shaman called him "Captain," I glanced at Chuck to catch his attention. This was a name that Chuck called Kenny, and hearing it spoken by the shaman startled me. The shaman now extended his wrinkly hand to Chuck. "Take this, Captain," he said. "You will need it more than your friend Steve will."

At first, I thought he was offering Chuck some sort of farewell trinket, that this was some kind of spiritual ritual. Chuck grasped the shaman's hand and the shaman pulled back quickly. When Chuck opened his palm, it was empty. The old man hadn't given Chuck a thing. I felt creepy about the whole exchange and just wanted to get out of there.

Thirty minutes later we were in the ditch.

When we left the bar, it was a dusky 6:30 p.m. and Chuck decided to take a country road to avoid the much busier highway. Sitting behind Chuck on the bike, we saw three antelope leaping across a ditch in the distance. "Hey, look," I shouted to him. Then I turned to my right to see if there were any more around, and in that split second, I found a pair of eyes at my shoulder. They belonged to a full-grown antelope.

The bike screeched when we drove right through the antelope at eighty miles per hour. Chuck was amazing, and I'll never know how he kept from dropping the bike. Being a helicopter pilot, he knew not to overreact. He didn't slam on the brakes as I might have done. He held the handlebars, tightened his arms, and maintained control of the motorcycle without wiping out. I believe he saved our lives.

That's not to say that we didn't swerve and spin all over the road. We did. When Chuck finally got the bike to a safe stop at the side of the road, I looked at my leg; I couldn't feel it. It just felt weird. Numb.

We found ourselves in the middle of an empty prairie road. Chuck couldn't find his cell phone and I didn't have mine. Our biker friends, Steve and George, traveling faster than we were, must have been way ahead of us. I only knew that we were somewhere near Broadus, Montana, near the junction of the Powder and Little Powder rivers. Earlier when looking at the map, I had jokingly called this tiny town of about 450 people "Badass." Now it wasn't funny, as we truly were the only ones around. We were hurt more than we first realized and the antelope that jumped in front of us was dead.

We just sat for a few minutes. Stunned. Chuck finally had the presence of mind to say, "We've got to get off the bike. We've got to get off the road." The road was narrow, and although we were off to the side, it still felt like we were in a very dangerous place since it was growing dark.

I looked at Chuck and noticed for the first time that his leg was twisted in the wrong way. *Oh, my God*, I thought. *He's in worse shape than I am. I need to help him.*

"We've got to get off the road," Chuck repeated, and he was more insistent this time, but I misunderstood and thought he meant to get off the Harley.

I still couldn't feel my leg and I tried to jump off. The clumsy movement made us fall over hard and the bike pinned us both on the rough pavement. "We have to get off the road!" Chuck shouted again. We wiggled out from under the bike, leaving it on the side of the road along with the dead antelope, and crawled off into the ditch.

After some time, I could see a vehicle in the distance. I began to wave and holler. The speeding car whizzed by and didn't stop. Didn't seem to notice our abandoned bike or me waving from the ditch. No one knew we were there.

I was in shock and the facts are hazy in my memory, but at some point, I flagged down a car and some people waited with us. Maybe someone called an ambulance—I'm not sure. Almost two hours later, some firemen happened to pass and stopped and gave us a blanket. They said because they weren't paramedics they couldn't take care of us, but they promised to send help. Chuck kept asking for his cell phone; he wanted to call for a helicopter.

By this time, a few others had stopped and gotten out of their cars and trucks. I remember a woman in the shadows covering me with the blanket. She asked, "Do you have any children?"

"Yes, I have two girls," I told her.

"Think about your children," she instructed me.

I didn't know why she would be saying this, which terrified me. "Am I dying and I don't know it?"

"Think about your children," she repeated.

To this day, I have no idea who she was, but I do know that she cared and I'm grateful that she did.

An ambulance arrived and took us to the local hospital. Chuck's condition was critical. His leg was crushed. My injuries were broken bones. The paramedics insisted on giving me strong pain medicine, but I kept saying, "No, no, no!" I thought it was important to be coherent so that I could make correct choices for both Chuck and me. It was clear that he was in bad shape.

In the ambulance, it began to sink in what had happened to us and I started to panic. I wish I knew who the driver and attendant were so that I could thank them, because they had to put up with a lot of hysterics from me. I was losing it. "Oh, my God," I sobbed. "The last time I was in an ambulance I lost Kenny. Here I am again in an ambulance.

I won't lose Chuck. Please don't let him die! Please don't let him die!"

We arrived at the hospital and the medical technicians began taking x-rays of my leg. A young doctor tried giving me Demerol. "I don't want that," I told him. The doctor was persistent, but I was even more stubborn. "I won't take it," I insisted. As a Canadian, I'd heard nightmares about the medical system in the United States. How the exorbitant costs could bankrupt you. *How am I going to afford this?* I wondered. *I could lose my house. My business. I could lose everything. I am not telling anybody that I'm in pain. How am I going to pay for this cast? What did those x-rays cost? Don't use the Kleenex; I've heard they charge a lot for that too.*

This kid doctor would not back down. He went and found an older physician, as if he went off to find his dad, and said, "Can you please tell her she needs to take this medicine?" The older doctor said, "No, she doesn't need it if she says she doesn't want it." I'd won that round.

The long night was an ongoing circus, a true nightmare, but the entire time I only wanted to know how Chuck was. I had to watch over Chuck.

As it happened, the surgeon on call had been drinking and wasn't able to come in. Chuck needed emergency surgery so we had to be transferred to another hospital. We were driven by ambulance 150 miles to Rapid City, South Dakota.

"Get me my phone," Chuck kept demanding. "Get me a helicopter." Unfortunately, his phone had gone missing, and because Chuck was in shock they thought he was babbling about the helicopter.

I tried to stand up for him. "He can pay for a helicopter," I explained. "He's a helicopter pilot. So why will no one go and find this man a helicopter?" Whatever Chuck wanted, I wanted for him. No one took us seriously and the request was ignored.

After a series of surgeries in Rapid City, lasting through the night and the next morning, Chuck was finally resting in his room. On top of everything, a cheery nurse burst through the door and I swear she announced to Chuck, "It's time to get you up and moving."

"Are you serious?" I questioned in disbelief. "He's been in surgery all night! He just came out of his sixth surgery! He can't move!"

"No, that's not right," she argued with me. "He had surgery two days ago." The nurse turned away from me and addressed Chuck directly, as if to leave me out of it. "We've got to get you up and walking."

For a moment, I thought she was right and I had lost my mind, or at least all sense of time, but one look at Chuck and I knew the nurse was mistaken. I also knew that Chuck was not ready for this, no matter how much time had gone by.

"You are not taking him out of this bed!" I yelled. And that nurse would have had to fight me off before she ever laid a hand on Chuck.

The incompetence was unbelievable and it frightened me. I planted myself in the chair next to Chuck's bed and would not leave. For ten days, I lived, slept, and ate in that chair. I watched what they did and how they did it. No one was going to harm Chuck.

I'd been in touch daily with my girls. I kept calling to make sure they were doing well. They were with their regular babysitter and felt safe. She made sure they were keeping up with their activities and schoolwork. I assured them that I was fine. We didn't let Chuck's mother or father know right away about his condition. His mother had just had a hip replacement and we didn't want to alarm her.

My rental business was on hold, running at minimum capacity, but I would not leave Chuck. Around the tenth day of our hospital stay, Chuck's mom and dad did arrive. His mom was still recuperating from her own surgery, but nothing was going to keep her from checking in on her son. Nothing would keep her from taking him home.

In the airport, we must have been quite a sight, the three of us rolling along in our wheelchairs. But in time, all three of us would be all right. Chuck and I went back to Utah with his parents. Shortly after, I went back to Canada to be with my girls.

At the hospital, we'd been known as the "miracle bikers."

"You must have an angel looking out for you two," more than one doctor told us. "It's a miracle you survived."

I couldn't help but recall the shaman who had told us to have a safe ride. He'd started to offer Chuck something, but then hadn't. At least that was how it appeared. He'd seemed creepy to me, and at first, I thought he might have put some kind of weird jinx on us, something to cause the accident. Later, I wondered about another possibility. Something more positive. He'd called Chuck "Captain." That's what Kenny answered to, and maybe, just maybe, Kenny was looking out for us. Maybe that's why we survived. Who can say?

Our bones were crushed and broken and bruised. A titanium rod held Chuck's leg together, but our hearts were strong. We were truly grateful to be alive. We left South Dakota with an unbreakable commitment to each other.

Adversity in life doesn't stop. We all face multiple obstacles. Annoyances and accidents still happen. Challenges, both large and small, continually present themselves in the workplace and in your personal life. If there is any trick to staying strong, to overcoming the obstacles that stand in your way, it's to surround yourself with those who uplift you, who will stand by you. These allies might be your family, they might not. They may be with you for life or they may appear for a brief moment, like the woman who comforted me on the side of the road when I was in trouble. If you do not have these kinds of people in your life, people whom you respect and love, go out and find them, or let them find you. You don't have to face everything alone.

CHAPTER 13

MORE THAN JUST EXISTENCE

For one year, Chuck needed to be in a wheelchair or on crutches. As you can imagine, living in two different countries was difficult for us, especially when I felt he needed my help. I spent that year bouncing back and forth from British Columbia to Utah. The girls stayed with their father on occasion, though more often my mother and the girls' babysitter were the people who came forward to help, and stayed with the girls in our home.

I would go to Utah for a week at a time, to cook, clean, and drive Chuck to work. Then I would return home to White Rock to cook, clean, and manage my own family and work responsibilities. Somehow it all got juggled. The gift shop was a success and my rental houses were booked.

In Utah, I took an interest in Chuck's business, headquartered in Salt Lake City. I didn't want to be known as the boss's girlfriend—barging in, stepping on everyone's toes. Still, it was impossible not to notice that the office walls were pink! The place was full of junky desks and the floor was covered in ten-year-old carpet. To say the office was dated would be an understatement. I thought this working environment had to be bad for morale. So I got busy. I remodeled the space into something that was contemporary—with slate floors, modern furniture, and a salt-water fish tank. It gave the place a much-needed facelift.

While I was in and out of the office, I began to notice other things. There were a few employees who were taking advantage, using company supplies for personal use. This wasn't petty. I'm not talking about pocketing an extra pencil here and there. This was big-time abuse, so I began giving Chuck some suggestions about how he might deal with it.

I also noticed that the marketing for new customers was not all it could be, and I eventually volunteered to do marketing, while trying not to step on any of the employees' toes. Again, I didn't want to be the obnoxious girlfriend sticking her nose where it didn't belong, but I did want Chuck's company to reach its potential. Sure, it was a good company, but I thought it could grow.

I started to market in states where the company didn't already have business. Places like Oregon and Washington. It took time to get any real support from Chuck's partner and the veteran employees, but I was able to help land new contracts that brought in money and enough extra work that the company hired sixty more people and opened two more offices. After that, I was accepted and respected.

There were other ways in which I became valuable. I knew customer service inside and out, skills developed long ago with Filter Queen and Mary Kay, and then with running my bed-and-breakfast and rental homes for so many years. I knew how to make a client happy.

At the time, Chuck's company had a very unhappy client, and as a result, the company was about to lose one of its major contracts.

"Let me speak to the man," I said to Chuck.

"Go for it!" I knew Chuck meant it. He not only saw my potential to handle the problem but also trusted me.

So I flew to Texas to meet with the dissatisfied client.

Our meeting was scheduled for 1:00 p.m. I called forty minutes early to confirm. "I just wanted to let you know that I'm already at the airport Marriott," I said to the client, "and I look forward to our meeting."

"What airport?" he demanded.

"Dallas/Fort Worth," I assured him, "where we are to meet at 1:00 p.m."

"You're at the wrong airport!" he barked back in a hostile tone. He clearly thought I was an idiot to have come to the wrong airport—that this was just one more problem he could add to his list of complaints against Chuck's company. "Just forget it!" he snarled. "You'll never make it here on time."

But I pushed back. "No, I don't want to just forget it," I

said. "We have an appointment and I will be there." I didn't want to let Chuck down, and I really did want to fix the issues that this man had. "Give me an hour. Just one hour and I'll make this right!"

He begrudgingly agreed to the hour (essentially twenty minutes past our meeting time, since I'd been forty minutes early). I knew he thought I'd never make it, would not give me one extra minute, and was now hoping that I would fail, just to prove he was right about his larger issues with the company.

For more than a year, I'd had a hundred-dollar bill in my wallet for emergencies. Now was the time to use it. When I got into the taxi, I waved the bill at the driver. "This is yours if you can get me to Love Field Airport in forty minutes."

The cab driver was up for the challenge. Although our destination was only about twenty-five miles away, the traffic was bad. But my driver had a plan. He drove fast, weaving in and out of the busy traffic like the old-time New York City cabbies you see in movies. I was terrified. I closed my eyes and trusted the cabbie, my new ally. I had to get to that appointment!

And I did. I arrived with enough time to sit down, brush my hair, open my briefcase, get out a bottle of water, sit back, and look as though I was relaxed and ready to go. Then the angry client walked in. He was surprised to see me.

He recited a long list of complaints. I listened carefully and then listened more. I let him talk without interruption until he had gotten everything out in the open. My Filter Queen and Mary Kay days had taught me how important it was to let the client know you cared—to let him know that he was being heard.

"Give me thirty days to solve your problems," I proposed.

I think he was impressed that I not only made the meeting but also took the time to understand. He gave me the thirty days to remedy the situation, and in the end, we did not lose the contract. We were able to convert him to a satisfied customer.

After two years of bouncing back and forth between Canada and the United States and working very hard with Chuck, I decided to leave my life in Canada and join Chuck permanently. The question I asked myself was *Why not?* The answer seemed obvious. There was no reason not to try.

I sold everything—my house and my businesses. I left friends and family to make the move to Utah. At the time, Carmen was a senior in high school and she was not comfortable with the move. She hated to leave her friends. It was not lost on me that I was forced to move far away during my high school years. I understood Carmen's concerns and decided to let her remain in Canada, where she stayed with a girlfriend's family. Caitlin, in the seventh grade, didn't have the same ties as her older sister, and she happily came with me.

Not everything went smoothly. Larry tried to make one last bit of trouble for me. He threatened to have us stopped at the border. Though he seldom made time to see his daughters, he wanted to make it difficult for me to have a new life. Thankfully, the threats were idle.

Now, a decade later, Chuck and I are happily married, our company continued to prosper until we sold it recently, and my daughters have grown into beautiful young women. They are university educated, confident, and thriving. Carmen attends veterinary school and Caitlin attends university and has her own business. Like me, she has an entrepreneurial spirit.

Wounds of the past have healed. My mother and father have long ago put their troubles behind them and are enjoying their retirement, and my younger sister, Brenda, and I remain as close as ever.

A psychic told me that I was meant to have two soul mates in my life. "You've lost one," she said, "but you've found another." At first, I wondered how that could be possible. Whether you believe in psychic intuition or not, I do think it's true that one can move forward after a crushing loss or deep disappointment. You do deserve to be happy, and you don't have to feel guilty about it. It's all up to you.

Chuck is a man of integrity and a talented businessman. I've learned so much from him. I noticed early on that he never looks back; he doesn't dwell in the past. "It is what it is," he'll say to me.

What I love most is that Chuck and I are a team, in business and in marriage. We like to work and we make it a priority to have fun. We support each other. Before we sold our company, we managed to quadruple our business. When I started working with Chuck, we had seventy-five employees. Eventually, we grew into a company that employed 400 people and expanded into thirty-eight states. I became director of operations, then vice president, and then president. Finally, due to our successes, I became CEO, moving Chuck out of his CEO role up to chairman of the board. Our company has been named six times as the fastest-growing company by the Utah Top 100. Not bad for a girl from the prairie!

We now divide our time between several homes and a ranch where we raise Kobe cattle.

Life is very good! I feel incredibly blessed and fortunate.

As you now know, I have gone through some tough, uncertain, and painful times. I survived a difficult childhood, an unhealthy marriage, the death of a partner I deeply loved, a serious motorcycle accident, and much more. I've felt the heaviness of sorrow and fear. I have felt stuck, alone, and lost.

I wanted to tell my story so that I could share with others how *it is possible* to move from a life of scarcity and being afraid—from a day-to-day existence of just getting by—to a happy life of abundance, security, contentment, and love.

To accomplish this, it takes a commitment to hard work, a belief in yourself, and the determination of never accepting no for an answer. When you are persistent, you can achieve what you need and want. Make a plan, have a goal, and stick with it, but then don't be afraid to revise or abandon that same plan when it no longer serves you. Learn to be spontaneous. Let yourself have fun.

And when your life *does* become better, don't be so naïve as to think that the challenges and obstacles will no longer confront you. There are always roadblocks. They never stop. That's just life, but you can learn not to let them paralyze you. Don't let challenges keep you from going where you want to go. No doubt you will encounter people along the way who will try to take you down or keep you stuck. There will be those who will help you as well. Remember to accept their gifts.

You have to fight to get where you want to go. That doesn't mean picking fights with others; it means not giving up, not letting others confine you to a restricted box. It might take you twenty tries, but if you keep at it, there is always a way.

So here are my questions for you:

Instead of just surviving, can you thrive?
Can you do more than just exist?

I hope your answer will be a loud and enthusiastic

Why not?

ACKNOWLEDGMENTS

I am so fortunate for my beautiful daughters, Carmen and Caitlin. You both inspire me with hope and strength. Because of you, I stay positive and move forward regardless of how unpleasant or difficult a situation may seem. Through thick and thin, you are both with me, always.

Carmen, thank you for giving me words of courage: "You always know the right thing to do. Just do it!" If it hadn't been for those words, I am not sure to this day whether I would have made the difficult choice that we all needed in order to improve our lives.

Caitlin, when I was sad and crying, thank you for helping me sleep during the night and staying by my side reassuring me that we would all be fine. I will be forever grateful for your support.

Chuck, my beloved husband, you've encouraged me to do what I know is best for me. With unconditional love, you always will be my best friend and soul mate. Thank you for giving me the strength to be who I am, and for always being there for me.

My dear mother, I understand now that you had to survive through many tough times—especially in a time period when divorce was not acceptable. You had to do what you believed was necessary. Thank you for being strong and setting an example, and for being not only my mother but also my friend.

Brenda, we always have each other. Thank you for being a wonderful sister. I will always be flying higher than an eagle and be the wind beneath your wings.

Jon, thank you for your friendship and for helping me bring this book into being.

To the members of my extended family and to my friends, know how much I appreciate all of you and that you have all impacted my life.

A NOTE FROM CATHY

There are many women, and men, too, who feel trapped, dominated, and unhappy. You are not alone. I, too, have been in this place. I hope my story has inspired and encouraged you to take a leap of faith, to trust that you can become your best self, that you can create a life of well-being—a life of security and emotional balance.

I have worked hard to turn these knocks I've had in life into opportunity and I am available to share my experiences and my hard-learned business and life lessons with you.

I'd love to hear your story.

You can reach me at www.CathyCode.com.

The person who says it cannot be done
should not interrupt the person doing it.

—CHINESE PROVERB

ABOUT THE AUTHOR

Cathy Code has thirty years of experience as an entrepreneur, business developer, and keynote speaker specializing in executive leadership. Cathy's leadership skills have led to her holding positions of director, president, or CEO in many industries. *Why Not? Survive and Thrive* is her first book.

MAKE NOTE OF YOUR "WHY NOT?"
MOMENTS AND GOALS

Why Not?

Why Not?